United States
Department of
Agriculture

**Forest
Service**

**North Central
Research Station**

**General Technical
Report NC-265**

POLICIES FOR MANAGING URBAN GROWTH AND LANDSCAPE CHANGE:

A KEY TO CONSERVATION IN THE 21ST CENTURY

David N. Bengston
Technical Editor

Papers presented at a symposium on "Policies for Managing Urban Growth and Landscape Change: A Key to Conservation in the 21st Century" at the Society for Conservation Biology 2004 Annual Meeting, *Conservation in an Urbanizing World*, Columbia University, New York, NY, July 30-August 2, 2004.

Bengston, David N., tech. ed. 2005. Policies for managing urban growth and landscape change: a key to conservation in the 21st century. Gen. Tech. Rep. NC-265. St. Paul, MN: U.S. Department of Agriculture, Forest Service, North Central Research Station. 51 p.

Protecting natural areas in the face of urbanization is one of the most important challenges for conservation in the 21st century. The papers in this collection examine key issues related to growth management and selected approaches to managing urban growth and minimizing its social and environmental costs. They were presented at the 2004 annual meeting of the Society for Conservation Biology; July 30-August 2, 2004; Columbia University, New York, NY.

KEY WORDS: Urban growth, urban sprawl, open space, landscape change, public policies, smart growth, brownfields redevelopment, sustainability.

Cover photo courtesy of
Greg Hove • City Forester • Eagan, MN

TABLE OF CONTENTS

ABOUT THE AUTHORS

David N. Bengston is a research social scientist and ecological economist with the USDA Forest Service, North Central Research Station in St. Paul, Minnesota, and an adjunct professor in the College of Natural Resources at the University of Minnesota. He is the Coordinator of the Ecological Economics in Forestry Research Group of the International Union of Forestry Research Organizations and was a 2004 Research Fellow with the Organisation for Economic Cooperation & Development. Dr. Bengston's research focuses on three areas: changing environmental attitudes, beliefs, and values; public policies for managing urban growth; and the environmental views and concerns of ethnic minority communities.

Brian Czech is a certified wildlife biologist and an adjunct professor at Virginia Polytechnic Institute and State University (Northern Center, Alexandria, Virginia). He is also president of the Center for the Advancement of the Steady State Economy (www.steadystate.org) based in Arlington, Virginia; chairman of The Wildlife Society's Working Group for the Steady State Economy, and a conservation biologist in civil service. Dr. Czech is the author of *Shoveling Fuel for a Runaway Train* (University of California Press 2002) and, with Paul R. Krausman, *The Endangered Species Act: History, Conservation Biology, and Public Policy* (Johns Hopkins University Press 2001).

David P. Fan is a professor in the Department of Genetics, Cell Biology and Development and an adjunct professor of Journalism and Mass Communication at the University of Minnesota and is president of InfoTrend, Inc. His research interests include computer content analysis of text, graphical data analysis, and mathematical time trend modeling of the impact of persuasive information on public knowledge, attitudes, and behaviors. Dr. Fan is the author of *Predictions of Public Opinion from the Mass Media: Computer Content Analysis and Mathematical Modeling* (Greenwood Press 1988).

Edward G. Goetz is professor and director, Urban and Regional Planning Program, Humphrey Institute of Public Affairs, University of Minnesota, Minneapolis. Dr. Goetz specializes in housing and local community development planning and policy. His research focuses on issues of race and poverty and their affects on housing policy planning and development. Dr. Goetz is the author of *Clearing the Way: Deconcentrating the Poor in Urban America* (Urban Institute Press 2003) and *Shelter Burden: Local Politics and Progressive Housing Policy* (Temple University Press 1993), and he is the co-editor of *The New Localism: Comparative Urban Politics in a Global Era* (Sage Publications 1993).

Jeffrey M. Levengood is a research scientist with the Center for Wildlife and Plant Ecology at the Illinois Natural History Survey in Champaign, Illinois. Dr. Levengood's work includes the nesting ecology and contaminant exposure of Lake Calumet black-crowned night herons; a comparative investigation of contaminants in fishes from the Calumet region of Chicago; transfer of contaminants from sediments to insectivorous birds via emergent aquatic insects; and patterns of contaminant exposure in unionid mussels from the Mississippi/Illinois Rivers confluence area.

Robert S. Potts is currently a forest planner on the Santa Fe National Forest in Santa Fe, New Mexico. Dr. Potts was previously a research ecologist with the USDA Forest Service, North Central Research Station's Forestry Sciences Lab in Rhinelander, Wisconsin. His research and professional interests include social assessment, knowledge management, science and technology application, and collaborative planning.

David Soucek is an aquatic ecotoxicologist with the Center for Ecological Entomology at the Illinois Natural History Survey in Champaign, Illinois. His work focuses on the effects of environmental contaminants on invertebrate populations and communities. Dr. Soucek's research involves the use of integrative (i.e., chemical, toxicological, and ecological) techniques to assess anthropogenic impacts on benthic macroinvertebrate communities; stressor identification/causality; laboratory-to-field validation; and incorporation of multiple levels of biological organization as endpoints in toxicological studies.

Roderick H. Squires is an associate professor in the Department of Geography and a member of the Conservation Biology faculty at the University of Minnesota. He is the co-editor of *Protecting the Land: Conservation Easements, Past, Present and Future* (Island Press 2000). In his teaching and research, he examines (1) how governments influence the behavior of individuals and corporations, especially behavior related to land ownership and land use, and (2) how individuals and corporations behave in response to such government action, using the land surface and subsurface, water, wildlife, and air.

Douglas F. Stotz is a conservation ecologist in the Office of Environmental and Conservation Programs at the Field Museum of Natural History in Chicago. His research interests focus on diversity patterns, biogeography, ecology, and conservation of birds. His field studies on birds have taken him through most of Mexico and South America, particularly Brazil, Bolivia, and Peru. In the United States he has done research on the ecology of birds in Arizona, Florida, and Illinois. In Illinois his research has been focused on migration and breeding birds along the Chicago lakefront, in the Lake Calumet area, Palos, and Midewin. Dr. Stotz is co-author of *Neotropical Birds: Ecology and Conservation* (University of Chicago Press 1996).

Youn Yeo-Chang is a professor in the Department of Forest Sciences and director of the Laboratory of Ecological Economics and Forest Policy at Seoul National University, Seoul, Republic of Korea. Major themes of his research include environmental accounting in forestry, forest sector analysis, international trade in forest products, and forest policy history. Dr. Youn has carried out collaborative research projects with international research institutions including the University of Tokyo, Louisiana State University, and the Center for International Forestry Research.

Alaka Wali is an anthropologist, John Nuveen Associate Curator and Director of the Center for Cultural Understanding and Change at the Field Museum of Natural History, Chicago. Dr. Wali's research program has concentrated on understanding the impact of global economic restructuring on the ways in which people organize themselves and constitute their social identities. She intends to use the results of the research to formulate more humane solutions to social problems. This research has taken place in Central and South American "hinterlands" and urban areas in the United States. Dr. Wali also is interested in exploring the obstacles and opportunities for anthropologists to disseminate what they know about culture to the general public.

Lynne M. Westphal is a research social scientist and project leader with the USDA Forest Service, North Central Research Station, in Evanston, Illinois. Dr. Westphal conducts and coordinates research to improve our understanding of the effects of urban natural resources (e.g., trees, rivers and wetlands, parks) on quality of life in urban areas. She is currently managing a multipartner research program focusing on the Rustbelt landscape of the Calumet Region of Illinois and Indiana. This suite of research projects will help policymakers and managers guide the economic and ecological revitalization of this area.

Gabor Zovanyi is a professor in the Department of Urban and Regional Planning, Eastern Washington University, Spokane, Washington. His specialties include growth management, sustainable development, environmental planning, land use regulations, land use law, and comparative urbanization. During the fall of 2001 Dr. Zovanyi visited New Zealand to carry out research related to growth management and sustainability initiatives in that country. Dr. Zovanyi continues to focus his research on relationships between growth management and sustainable development, following the direction set by his 1998 book, *Growth Management for a Sustainable Future: Ecological Sustainability as the New Growth Management Focus for the 21st Century* (Praeger).

FOREWORD

Protecting natural areas in the face of urbanization is one of the most important challenges for conservation in the 21st century. Rapid population growth and increasingly land-consumptive development patterns have combined in many countries to put severe pressure on natural systems. In the United States, sprawling development is the most significant factor affecting forest ecosystems in the South (Wear and Greis 2002) and is the leading cause of habitat loss and species endangerment in the contiguous U.S. (Czech et al. 2000). Forest Service Chief Dale Bosworth (2004) has identified loss of open space due to sprawling development as one of the four main threats to public and private forests.

The public sector has responded to growing awareness of and concern about the social, economic, and environmental costs of sprawling development by creating a wide range of policy instruments designed to more effectively manage urban growth. Growth management has been defined in many ways, but essentially it consists of government actions "… to guide the location, quality, and timing of development" (Porter 1997: vii). The papers in this collection examine key issues related to growth management and selected approaches to managing urban growth and minimizing its undesirable impacts. They were presented at a symposium on "Policies for Managing Urban Growth and Landscape Change: A Key to Conservation in the 21st Century" at the Society for Conservation Biology 2004 Annual Meeting, *Conservation in an Urbanizing World*, held on the campus of Columbia University in New York on July 30 through August 2, 2004.

In the increasingly urbanized world in which we live – with about 80 percent of the United States population currently living in urban and suburban areas – natural resource planners, managers, and policymakers need a better understanding of the context and impacts of urban sprawl and the range of policy instruments available to manage urban growth as they work with professionals from many other fields to deal with the threats posed by development. The papers in this collection will contribute to building that understanding.

LITERATURE CITED

Bosworth, D. 2004. Is America on track toward sustainable forests? Pages 3-5, Proceedings, Society of American Foresters 2003 Annual Convention, Forest Science in Practice. SAF Publication 04-01. Buffalo, NY, October 25-29, 2003. Bethesda, MD: Society of American Foresters. 426 p.

Czech, B.; Krausman, P.R.; Devers, P.K. 2000. Economic associations among causes of species endangerment in the United States. BioScience. 50(July): 593-601.

Porter, D.R. 1997. Managing growth in America's communities. Washington, DC: Island Press. 311 p.

Wear, D.N.; Greis, J.G. 2002. Southern Forest Resource Assessment: summary of findings. Journal of Forestry. 100(7): 6-14.

THE RISE AND FALL OF CONCERN ABOUT URBAN SPRAWL IN THE UNITED STATES: AN UPDATED ANALYSIS

David P. Fan,[1] David N. Bengston,[2] Robert S. Potts,[3] Edward G. Goetz[4]

ABSTRACT—An indicator of public concern about urban sprawl is presented, based on computer content analysis of public discussion in the news media from 1995 through 2004. More than 50,000 news stories about sprawl were analyzed for expressions of concern. Overall concern about sprawl grew rapidly during the latter half of the 1990s. Concern about the environmental impacts of sprawl was most salient, followed by loss of farmland and traffic problems. Attention to urban sprawl began to decline in 2000 and has leveled off in recent years.

Urban sprawl may be characterized as relatively low-density, noncontiguous, automobile-dependent, residential and non-residential development that converts and consumes relatively large amounts of farmland and natural areas (Burchell *et al.* 1998). Concern about sprawl is not new, but the intensity and the nature of the discussion has evolved over time. In recent years, urban sprawl has been linked to an array of economic and social costs, including higher costs for providing public infrastructure such as roads and utilities, more vehicle miles traveled and less cost-efficient transit, as well as a variety of negative quality of life and social impacts (Burchell *et al.* 1998). The environmental costs of sprawl are becoming increasingly clear. Of particular concern to natural resource professionals, sprawl has been identified as the most significant factor affecting forest ecosystems in the southern United States (Wear and Greis 2002). In North Carolina, for example, forest cover has declined by more than 1.0 million acres (about 5 percent) since 1990, and urban development is the predominant cause of the net loss (Brown 2004). Further, sprawling development has been implicated as the leading cause of habitat loss and species endangerment in the mainland United States (Czech *et al.* 2000).

Public concern about the social and environmental impacts of sprawl has grown in recent years, as shown by a variety of indicators. For example, a series of five surveys commissioned by the Pew Center for Civic Journalism (2000) indicated that the negative effects of sprawl and growth are now edging out more traditional issues, such as crime, in terms of overall impact on the quality of life in local communities. This was a significant increase from a 1994 Pew Center poll. The increase in referenda and ballot measures on growth management, preservation of open space, and retention of farmland and historic resources is another indicator suggesting a surge in attention to sprawl and

interest in managing growth (Myers 1999, Myers and Puentes 2001). Finally, mounting interest in Smart Growth and other approaches to land management in the United States (Chen 2000, Weitz 1999), the rising number of local, regional, and national land trusts, and increases in the acreage conserved in land trusts (Land Trust Alliance 2001) also signal a shift in attitudes toward sprawl.

The focus on sprawl is germane to planners, managers, and policymakers involved in protecting urban, rural, and inter-face forests and other natural resources from urban encroachment. The level of public concern will influence the social and political acceptance of policies and programs such as the USDA Forest Service Forest Legacy Program (USDA FS 2002) aimed at protecting forests, including state forests (Williams *et al.* 2004). In the absence of data highlighting sprawl, planners will be hard pressed to develop politically acceptable management plans.

This paper describes an indicator of concern about the impacts of sprawl that allows policymakers and planners to monitor change in attitudes about sprawl.[5] This social indicator is based on computer content analysis of news media discussion about sprawl. Sprawl has sparked an extensive public debate in the United States in recent years. Analysis of news media content allows us to take the pulse of ongoing public debate about sprawl and to track change in the debate over time.

The role of the media in both shaping and reflecting public opinion on a wide range of social issues has been well documented (Fan 1988, 1997; Fan and Cook 2003; McCombs 2004; Page *et al.* 1987). Related studies have found that the news media also strongly influence agenda-setting for public policy issues, i.e., there is a relationship between the relative emphasis given by the media to issues and the degree of

[1] Genetics, Cell Biology, and Development, University of Minnesota, 250 Biological Sciences Center, 1445 Gortner Avenue, St. Paul, MN 55108; e-mail: dfan@cbs.umn.edu
[2] USDA Forest Service, North Central Research Station, 1992 Folwell Avenue, St. Paul, MN 55108; e-mail: dbengston@fs.fed.us
[3] USDA Forest Service, Santa Fe National Forest, 1474 Rodeo Road, Santa Fe, NM 87502-7114; e-mail: robertpotts@fs.fed.us
[4] Urban and Regional Planning Program, Humphrey Institute of Public Affairs, University of Minnesota, 301-19th Avenue South, Minneapolis, MN 55455; e-mail: egoetz@umn.edu
[5] This indicator of sprawl concern was first reported in Bengston, *et al.* (2005), which analyzed discussion about sprawl in the news media through the first quarter of 2001. This paper updates the sprawl time trends through the end of 2004.

Citation for proceedings: Bengston, David N., tech. ed. 2005. Policies for managing urban growth and landscape change: a key to conservation in the 21st Century. Gen. Tech. Rep. NC-265. St. Paul, MN: U.S. Department of Agriculture, Forest Service, North Central Research Station. 51 p.

salience these topics have for the public and political agendas. Dearing *et al.* (1996) and McCombs (2004) reviewed hundreds of published studies on media agenda-setting, the vast majority of which support the agenda-setting hypothesis. Therefore, analysis of the public debate about urban sprawl contained in the news media is not mere "media analysis" – it is a window onto the broader social debate and an indirect means for gauging public attitudes and concerns about sprawl.

The next section briefly describes the online data and computer content analysis method used in this study. The sections that follow describe the main concerns we identified and the variation in overall sprawl concern over time. We conclude with a discussion of the policy implications of these findings, and the relevance of this approach to planners, managers, and policymakers.

DATA AND METHODS

News media stories about urban sprawl were obtained from the LexisNexis™ commercial online database. The following search command was used to identify news stories about sprawl: (sprawl! w/p (urban! or suburb!)), where w/p means "within the same paragraph" and the exclamation point means that all trailing letters are permitted. This search turned up more than 51,000 stories, all of which were downloaded. Only text within 100 words of the search terms was downloaded. This greatly reduced the amount of irrelevant text that would have been retrieved from stories that mentioned sprawl only in passing.

The search resulted in 36,787 stories retrieved for the original analysis (Bengston *et al.* 2005) from January 1, 1995, through March 31, 2001, from 111 news sources: 94 local newspapers, 5 national newspapers, 6 national and regional newswires, and 6 television and radio news transcripts. Among these news sources, four local newspapers were omitted in the present update from April 1, 2001, through December 31, 2004, due to non-availability through the LexisNexis database. This loss of 3.6 percent of the news sources was likely to have a negligible effect on the results of the update. The update included an additional 14,684 stories for a total of 51,471.

Irrelevant stories that were not about urban sprawl were filtered out of the database using the InfoTrend™ software. The InfoTrend software can discard paragraphs that do not fit user-specified criteria. After we removed the irrelevant text, the final database included 50,688 stories.

The news stories were then examined to identify the most frequently expressed concerns about urban sprawl. Categories of concerns were not predetermined but emerged from analysis of the textual data. Given the large volume of text, we did not examine each story in the database. A random sample of about 500 stories was examined to identify specific concerns about sprawl. The specific concerns are described in the Findings and Discussion section.

Scoring the news stories for expressions of concern about sprawl was done with the InfoTrend computer content analysis method using the Filtscor computer language. An algorithm was developed to code the news stories for the number of paragraphs expressing each of the specific concerns about urban sprawl. If a paragraph contained more than one expression of the same sprawl concern, it was counted as only one expression of the concern. If a paragraph contained expressions of several different sprawl concerns, however, each of the concerns was counted once. A detailed description of the method used to code sprawl concerns is given in Bengston *et al.* (2005).

With traditional human-coded content analysis involving more than one coder, intercoder reliability is often a problem due to ambiguous coding instructions, cognitive differences among the coders, or random recording errors (Weber 1990). With the computer-coded approach used in this study, however, the computer always applies the coding rules consistently and therefore intercoder reliability is not an issue. But it is important to ensure that the computer instructions accurately code the concepts of interest. We examined a random sample of 500 stories that were coded using our computer instructions to determine whether the instructions were able to accurately identify expressions of each of the individual concerns about sprawl. After final refinements, the accuracy rates for the specific sprawl concerns ranged from 85 to 96 percent, and the overall accuracy rate for all nine concerns was 92 percent. Krippendorff (1980) suggests a minimum acceptable reliability of 80 percent as a rule of thumb in content analysis.

FINDINGS AND DISCUSSION

The public debate about sprawl has been lively and dynamic in recent years. News media accounts express a diversity of concerns about sprawl put forth by a wide range of stakeholders, and sprawl is clearly framed as a significant social and environmental problem. Sprawling patterns of development also have supporters, whose arguments are often based on private property rights and consumer sovereignty: consumers know what they want and should be free to exercise their choice in the marketplace. But the public discussion of sprawl has been largely opposed to it (Gillham 2002), and we found this to be true of the news media debate. Therefore, this analysis focuses on negative perceptions.

Nine Concerns About Sprawl

The following nine concerns about sprawl emerged most frequently in the news media analyzed. These nine concerns are the concepts that were coded and counted in this analysis. Each concern is followed by a quotation from a news story in our database expressing the particular concern.

1. Unspecified Concern is the view that sprawl is a problem, is undesirable, and should be avoided or stopped. This passage indicates that sprawl should be fought but gives no specific reasons:

As policy director, Rowen focused on issues that made up Norquist's agenda, "primarily transportation, land use and fighting urban sprawl" (Nichols 1998: A3).

2. Environmental Impacts is the concern that sprawl causes a wide range of environmental damage, such as loss of wildlife habitat, forest fragmentation, decreased air and water quality, and loss of biodiversity.

The painful concept of urban sprawl has become increasingly poignant as we witness the despoiling of countless acres of local forest in the name of "progress and prosperity" (Indianapolis Star 2000: D4).

3. Loss of Farmland is the concern that sprawl is responsible for the loss of farmland or is a threat to farmland. This concern also encompasses the loss of rural character and way of life.

The dilemma is a common one facing farmers in northern Illinois, where urban sprawl is gobbling up choice farmland at an unsustainable rate and encroaching on the agricultural way of life for those who remain (Parisi 1998: B5).

4. Loss of Open Space is the view that sprawl is responsible for the conversion of open space to developed uses or is a threat to open space. This concern may be related to *loss of farmland*, but was coded separately because it was often expressed as a distinct concern. In this study, open space is broadly defined to include all types of undeveloped land, such as fields, forests, farmland, parks, and wetlands.

I've lived the uncontrolled city planning (urban sprawl) and have seen acres of open land paved over. I've seen multiple cities become a blur because their city limits butt up against each other. And I've seen the friendliness of the people turn into a bare tolerance of others because everyone is elbow to elbow (Des Moines Register 1997: 7).

5. Traffic Problems is the concern that sprawl contributes to traffic congestion, longer commutes, road rage, and other traffic problems.

Sprawl has resulted in lengthier commutes, worsening traffic congestion and air pollution (Ibata 2000: 9D).

6. Urban Decline is the view that sprawl contributes to the decline of core cities due to public and private financial resources being dedicated to growth at the periphery instead of redevelopment and revitalization of urban centers.

The note of caution reported from the consultants that such improvements "might contribute to urban sprawl" and "might counter redevelopment efforts in the urban core" are brushed aside. Experience in city after city has shown, without any doubt, that these undesirable effects will in fact occur.... The urban core is a wasteland of vacant lots, abandoned buildings and surface parking lots. (Kansas City Star 2000: B6).

7. Taxpayer Subsidy is the view that sprawl does not pay its own way, is subsidized by taxpayers, and entails hidden costs. Sprawl subsidies include the cost of providing roads, municipal water, and sewer services; hidden costs include increased demand for schools, longer response times for police, fire, ambulance services, and so on.

Increased funding to preserve undeveloped land, to build parks in urban areas and to improve air quality are a good start, but they still don't address the fundamental cause of urban sprawl: the provision of a high quality of life at subsidized prices. (Barrett 1999: 3).

8. Loss of Community is the concern that sprawl destroys sense of community and sense of place, and fosters social isolation.

Polet believes neighborhood butcher shops are disappearing because of urban sprawl and zoning which discourage mixing small shops and homes in a neighborhood.... "They really need to re-evaluate their restrictions because there's no sense of community anymore" (Seelig 1998: F1).

9. Loss of Historic Sites is the view that sprawl threatens historic and culturally significant sites such as historic buildings, historic downtown areas, historic districts, and prehistoric sites.

It is not that change is bad, per se, but rather that Madison is experiencing so much change so very rapidly–in the form of population growth, new residential and commercial development and suburban sprawl–that some controls must be administered in order to preserve not just the past but the present. That is why any move that significantly weakens protections for historic structures must be seen as a wrongheaded assault on Madison's character (Capital Times 1997: 10A).

These nine concerns about sprawl are the most commonly expressed in the public debate contained in the news media. In addition, a variety of additional, infrequently mentioned concerns about sprawl were also expressed. Examples include the view that automobile-dependent development contributes to sedentary living habits and adversely affects human health; the view that subdivisions pushing farther out into wildlife habitat have contributed to increased incidence of rabies, rattlesnake bites, and other adverse human-wildlife encounters in some parts of the country; and the concern that sprawl complicates wildland fire management. But, to date, these concerns have been a small part of the overall discussion, and they were not included in this analysis.

Volume of Discussion About Sprawl

Figure 1 shows the number of news media stories about urban sprawl in our database from the first quarter of 1995 through the last quarter of 2004. News media discussion of sprawl concern grew from about 800 to 900 stories per quarter in 1995 and early 1996 to peaks of more than 2,200 stories each in 1999 (2,244 in the first quarter, and 2,220 in the fourth quarter). These peaks in sprawl discussion were due in part to Vice President Al Gore's championing a "livability agenda" and Smart Growth concepts. Gore officially launched the Livable Communities initiative on January 11, 1999, in a speech to the American Institute of Architects. A White House Task Force on Livable Communities was created in August 1999 to coordinate livable community policies across 18 executive branch agencies (Livable Communities 2000). Gore's strong support and frequent public discussion of smart growth and related concepts in late 1998 and 1999 appear to have intensified the national debate on sprawl.

Beginning in 2000, the number of stories about sprawl began a gradual decline, but remained at more than twice the volume of just 6 years earlier. In the second quarter of 2001, however, the volume of discussion began to drop significantly, falling to about 1,000 stories per quarter by the fourth quarter of 2001. News media discussion about the issue has remained close to this level in recent years, with about the same number of stories as were found in 1995 and 1996.

Figure 1.—Number of news media stories about sprawl, 1995-2004.

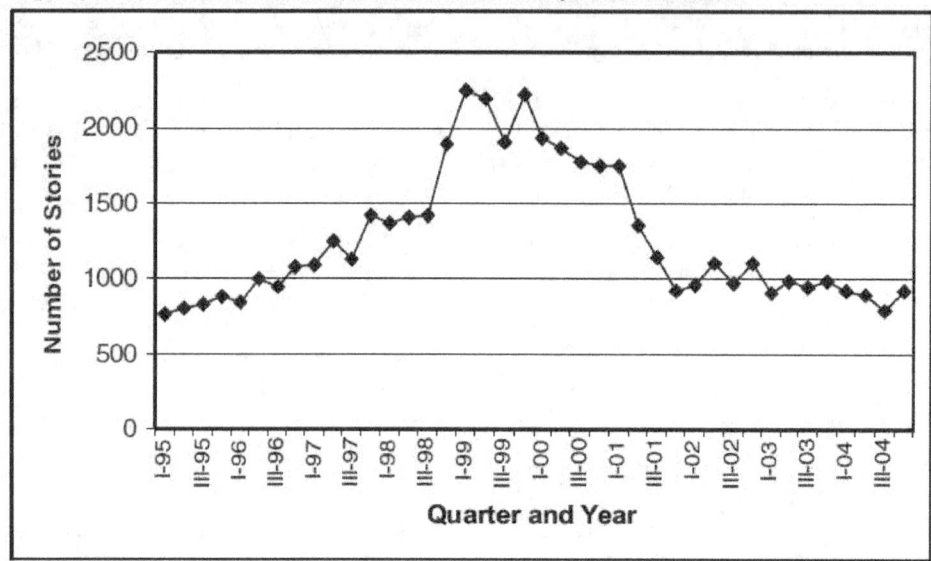

Ranking Concerns About Sprawl

About 46 percent of all the expressions of concern about sprawl were of general or *unspecified concern*. When the general category is excluded, the debate about sprawl in the United States has been dominated by concern about *environmental impacts* (fig. 2), accounting for 36 percent of all specific concerns over the entire time period. The prominence of press concern about environmental impacts is consistent with a national survey carried out in 2000 in which "loss of green spaces, forests and farmland" was ranked as the most significant problem (Penn, Schoen, and Berland Associates 2000).

Although environmental concerns are most prominent, other sprawl concerns also are important components of the public debate (fig. 2). In order of their frequency of expression, the other specific concerns were as follows: *loss of farmland* (19.3 percent), *traffic problems* (13.3 percent), *loss of open space* (12.8 percent), *urban decline* (7.1 percent), *taxpayer subsidy* (6.7 percent), *loss of community* (2.5 percent), and *loss of historic sites* (2.2 percent). Concern about *loss of farmland* has long been significant, particularly in smaller metropolitan areas in predominantly rural states. For example, farmland was number one on a list of the "Top ten things adversely affected by urban sprawl" compiled by 1000 Friends of Iowa.[6] A recent literature synthesis found consensus about the link between sprawl and loss of agricultural land (Burchell *et al.* 1998). This synthesis also found general agreement–albeit based on scant literature–about reduced regional open space in sprawl-dominated areas. Growing concern about traffic problems was indicated in a survey conducted in 2000 for Smart Growth America, which found that 54 percent of Americans believe traffic worsened over the previous 3 years in the area in which they live (Beldon, Russonello & Stewart, 2000). Concern about urban decline has been an important part of the debate about sprawl in certain large cities, although Downs (1999) found no statistically significant relationship between sprawl and urban decline.

Variation in Specific Concerns Over Time

We also analyzed shifts in the discussion about sprawl over time, i.e., changes in the relative emphasis of concerns. Figure 3 displays time trends for five of the eight specific concerns: *environmental impacts, loss of farmland, traffic problems, loss of open space,* and *urban decline.* The share of concern about *environmental impacts* gradually declined from 1995 through 1998 and then began to increase, peaking at 47 percent of all expressions of specific sprawl concerns in the second quarter of 2003. This pattern is almost the inverse of the trend in overall volume of news stories about urban sprawl (fig. 1). *Loss of farmland* gradually declined over time, except for the early volatile years. The shares of *traffic problems* and *loss of open space* followed similar patterns, rising throughout most of the first half of the 10-year time period and then gradually declining. The rise in expressions of concern about *traffic problems* and *loss of open space* during the late 1990s signaled a shift in the national debate toward these quality of life issues. Finally, concern about *urban decline* fell from 10 percent of all specific expressions of concern in 1995-96 to just 5.5 percent in 1999-2000. This may be due to the rapid economic growth of the late 1990s, in which urban economies fared comparatively well. Many large U.S. cities showed signs of renewal during this period, such as increased homeownership and decreased violent crime, unemployment, and poverty. The share of concern about *urban decline* then rose in 2001 and 2002 as the economy weakened.

CONCLUSIONS AND IMPLICATIONS

In recent years, urban sprawl has sparked an extensive public debate in the United States that will shape land use policy for years to come. This debate is captured in the news media discussion of sprawl. Our findings suggest that overall concern about sprawl grew rapidly during the latter half of the 1990s. This confirms Gillham's (2002: xiv) suggestion of a "gathering storm" of concern about the effects of urban sprawl. The

---

[6] 1000 Friends of Iowa is a nonprofit educational and advocacy organization that focuses on land use issues (www.kfoi.org).

Figure 2.—Specific concerns about sprawl as a percent of total expressions of concern, 1995-2004.

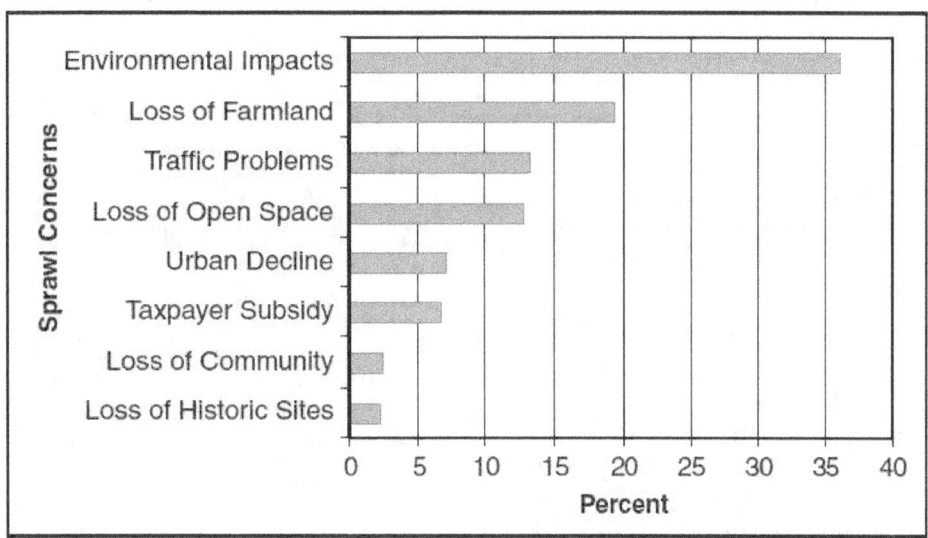

increase in concern found in our analysis corresponds with various indicators of changing attitudes toward sprawl mentioned earlier, such as public opinion polls in which sprawl is identified as one of the top concerns among residents of local communities and the steady growth of ballot box initiatives related to growth management in the late 1990s. After reaching a peak in 1999, concern about sprawl reflected in news media discussion began to decline and has leveled off in recent years.

Understanding the evolution of concerns about sprawl over time is important in designing effective response strategies. The national debate about sprawl has shifted over time and will likely continue to shift in the future. An awareness of the dynamics of the public debate about sprawl can help policymakers develop more socially acceptable strategies for managing growth that are consistent with the changing social landscape.

Figure 3.—Trends in expressions of selected concerns about sprawl, 1995-2004.

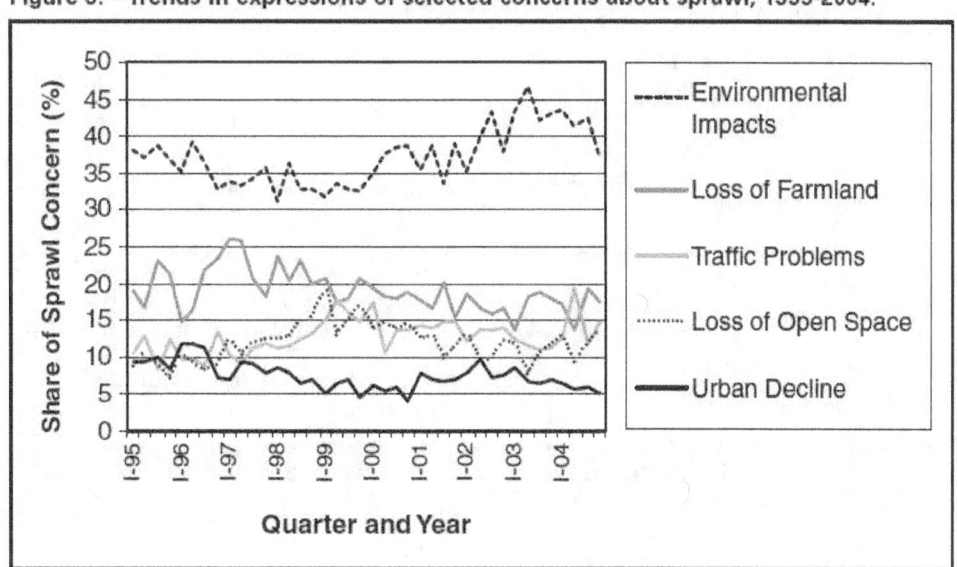

LITERATURE CITED

Barrett, J.P. 1999. Pro con: Is the urban sprawl initiative announced by the Clinton administration in January really needed? Pro: Any growth plan must address who pays for others "paradise." Milwaukee Journal Sentinel, March 14; Sect.: Crossroads: 3.

Belden, Russonello & Stewart, Inc. 2000. National survey on growth and land development (conducted for Smart Growth America). Washington, DC: Belden Russonello & Stewart, Inc. [Available online: http://www.smart-growthamerica.com/poll.pdf]

Bengston, D.N.; Potts, R.S.; Fan, D.P.; Goetz, E.G. 2005. An analysis of the public discourse about urban sprawl in the United States: monitoring concern about a major threat to forests. Forest Policy and Economics. 7(5): 745-756.

Brown, M.J. 2004. Forest statistics for North Carolina, 2002. Resource Bull. SRS-88. Asheville, NC: U.S. Department of Agriculture, Forest Service, Southern Research Station. [Available online: http://www.srs.fs.usda.gov/pubs/view-pub.jsp?index=6274]

Burchell, R.W.; Shad, N.A.; Listokin, D.; et al. 1998. The costs of sprawl – revisited. TCRP Report 39, Transit Cooperative Research Program, Transportation Research Board, National Research Council. Washington, DC: National Academy Press. 268 pp. [Available online: http://gulliver.trb.org/pub-lications/tcrp/tcrp_rpt_39-a.pdf]

Capital Times. 1997. Keep historic protections. Capital Times, (Madison, WI). December 2; Editorial: 10A.

Chen, D. 2000. The science of smart growth. Scientific American. 283(6): 84-91.

Czech, B.; Krausman, P.R.; Devers, P.K. 2000. Economic associations among causes of species endangerment in the United States. BioScience. 50(July): 593-601.

Dearing, J.W.; Rogers, E.M.; Chaffee, S.H. 1996. Agenda-setting (Communication Concepts, Vol. 6). Thousand Oaks, CA: Sage. 139 p.

Des Moines Register. 1997. Letters to the editor. Des Moines Register. November 23; Sect.: Opinion: 7.

Downs, A. 1999. Some realities about sprawl and urban decline. Housing Policy Debate. 10(4): 955-974.

Fan, D.P. 1988. Predictions of public opinion from the mass media: computer content analysis and mathematical modeling. New York: Greenwood Press. 202 p.

Fan, D.P. 1997. Computer content analysis of press coverage and prediction of public opinion for the 1995 sovereignty referendum in Quebec. Social Science Computer Review. 15(4): 351-366.

Fan, D.P.; Cook, R.D. 2003. A differential equation model for predicting public opinions and behaviors from persuasive information: application to the Index of Consumer Sentiment. Journal of Mathematical Sociology. 27(1): 29-51.

Gillham, O. 2002. The limitless city: a primer on the urban sprawl debate. Washington, DC: Island Press. 309 p.

Ibata, D. 2000. Builders warm to 'smart growth.' Chicago Tribune. October 15; Sect.: Real Estate: 9D.

Indianapolis Star. 2000. Suburban sprawl behind the mall. Indianapolis Star. July 2; Editorial: D4.

Kansas City Star. 2000. Letters, faxes and e-mails. Kansas City Star. October 5; Sect.: Opinion: B6.

Krippendorff, K. 1980. Content analysis: an introduction to its methodology. Newbury Park, CA: Sage. 189 p.

Land Trust Alliance. 2001. Millions of acres conserved by voluntary action; Number of nonprofit land trusts at new high. Land trust census press release, September 12, 2001. Washington, DC: Land Trust Alliance.

Livable Communities. 2000. Building livable communities: sustaining prosperity, improving quality of life, building a sense of community. Washington, DC: Livable Communities. For sale by the U.S. Government Printing Office. 68 p.

McCombs, M. 2004. Setting the agenda: the news media and public opinion. Cambridge, UK: Polity Press. 184 p.

Myers, P. 1999. Livability at the ballot box: state and local referenda on parks, conservation, and smarter growth, election day 1998. Discussion paper. Center on Urban and Metropolitan Policy. Washington, DC: The Brookings Institution. 17 p.

Myers, P.; Puentes, R. 2001. Growth at the ballot box: electing the shape of communities in November 2000. Discussion paper. Center on Urban and Metropolitan Policy. Washington, DC: The Brookings Institution. 128 p.

Nichols, M. 1998. Rowen to oversee Norquist's staff. Milwaukee Journal Sentinel. June 14: A3.

Page, B.I.; Shapiro, R.Y.; Dempsey, G.R. 1987. What moves public opinion? American Political Science Review. 81(1): 23-43.

Parisi, T. 1998. Urban sprawl harvesting prime farmland. State Journal-Register (Springfield, IL). February 1; Sect.: Business: B5.

Penn, Schoen and Berland Associates. 2000. Why voters care about the quality of life survey. Washington, DC: Penn, Schoen and Berland Associates, Inc. 31 p.

Pew Center for Civic Journalism. 2000. Straight talk from Americans, 2000: national survey results. Washington, DC: Pew Foundation. [Available online: http://www.pewcenter.org/doingcj/research/r_ST2000.html]

Seelig, F. 1998. Prime cuts. Grand Rapids (MI) Press. November 1; F1.

U.S. Department of Agriculture, Forest Service 2002. Forest Legacy Program Report for 2001. Washington, DC [Available online: http://www.fs.fed.us/cooperativeforestry/programs/loa/flp.shtml]

Wear, D.N.; Greis, J.G. 2002. Southern forest resource assessment. Gen. Tech. Rep. SRS-53. Ashville, NC: U.S. Department of Agriculture, Forest Service, Southern Research Station. [Available online: http://www.srs.fs.fed.us/sustain/]

Weber, R.P. 1990. Basic content analysis. (2nd ed.). Newbury Park, CA: Sage. 95 p.

Weitz, J. 1999. From quiet revolution to smart growth: state growth management programs, 1960-1999. Journal of Planning Literature. 14(2): 266-337.

Williams, D.; Gottfried, R.; Brockett, C.; Evans, J. 2004. An integrated analysis of the effectiveness of Tennessee's Forest Greenbelt Program. Landscape and Urban Planning. 69(2-3): 287-297.

Urbanization as a Threat to Biodiversity: Trophic Theory, Economic Geography, and Implications for Conservation Land Acquisition

Brian Czech[1]

ABSTRACT—Habitat loss is often cited as the primary cause of species endangerment in the United States, followed by invasive species, pollution, and direct take. Urbanization, one type of habitat loss, is the leading cause of species endangerment in the contiguous United States and entails a relatively thorough transformation from the "economy of nature" to the human economy. Principles of economic geography indicate that urbanization will continue as a function of economic growth, while principles of conservation biology indicate that the most thorough competitive exclusion occurs in urban areas. These findings suggest the need for an *ecologically* macroeconomic approach to conservation land acquisition strategies.

"Habitat loss" is often cited as the primary cause of species endangerment in the United States, followed by invasive species, pollution, disease, and direct take. However, various types of habitat loss are readily identified, such as logging, mining, agriculture, and urbanization (table 1). When these types of habitat loss are considered separate causes of species endangerment, invasive species are identified as the leading cause of species endangerment in the United States, including Hawaii and Puerto Rico (Czech et al. 2000). On the mainland United States, however, urbanization is the

Table 1.— Causes of endangerment for the first 877 (of the current 1,262) species in the United States and Puerto Rico classified as threatened or endangered by the United States Fish and Wildlife Service (from Czech et al. 2000).

Cause	Number of species endangered by cause
Interactions with nonnative species	305
Urbanization	275
Agriculture	224
Outdoor recreation and tourism development	186
Domestic livestock and ranching activities	182
Reservoirs and other running water diversions	161
Modified fire regimes and silviculture	144
Pollution of water, air, or soil	144
Mineral, gas, oil, and geothermal extraction or exploration	140
Industrial, institutional, and military activities	131
Harvest, intentional and incidental	120
Logging	109
Road presence, construction, and maintenance	94
Loss of genetic variability, inbreeding depression, or hybridization	92
Aquifer depletion, wetland draining or filling	77
Native species interactions, plant succession	77
Disease	19
Vandalism (destruction without harvest)	12

[1] Virginia Polytechnic Institute and State University, Northern Virginia Center, 1021 Prince Street, Alexandria, VA 22314; e-mail: brianczech@juno.com

Citation for proceedings: Bengston, David N., tech. ed. 2005. Policies for managing urban growth and landscape change: a key to conservation in the 21st Century. Gen. Tech. Rep. NC-265. St. Paul, MN: U.S. Department of Agriculture, Forest Service, North Central Research Station. 51 p.

leading cause of endangerment, although it may be overtaken by invasive species in the coming decades. Urbanization and nonnative species invasions are often related, because urbanization disturbs habitats, opens niches to invasive species, and leads to introduction (sometimes intentional) of invasive species.

In most cases of habitat loss, natural capital such as soil, water, timber, grass, or minerals is extracted and reallocated from the "economy of nature" (comprised of nonhuman species) to the human economy (fig 1). In the economy of nature, such natural capital had been used for producing nonhuman individuals and species (Czech 2000a). After its reallocation to the human economy, natural capital is used for producing human goods and services.

In some cases of habitat loss, natural capital is simply cleared away to make room for human economic infrastructure, enterprises, and residences, although some of the natural capital may be salvaged and used, on or offsite, in various economic sectors. This "liquidation" of natural capital is analogous to the tearing down of a warehouse and the disposal of its contents; some is used but much is simply destroyed and replaced (Daly 1996). Natural capital liquidation is often associated with reservoirs and water developments, road construction, and urbanization.

Urbanization is a common type of habitat loss that entails a relatively thorough transformation from the economy of nature to the human economy. The purpose of this paper is to summarize the impact of urbanization on species conservation in the United States and to analyze the impact of urbanization in the context of ecological trophic theory and basic principles of economic geography. A discussion of trophic theory and economic geography principles may help to shed light on management and policy implications for species conservation.

Figure 1.—Reallocation of natural capital from economy of nature to human economy in the process of economic growth. Modified from Czech (2000a).

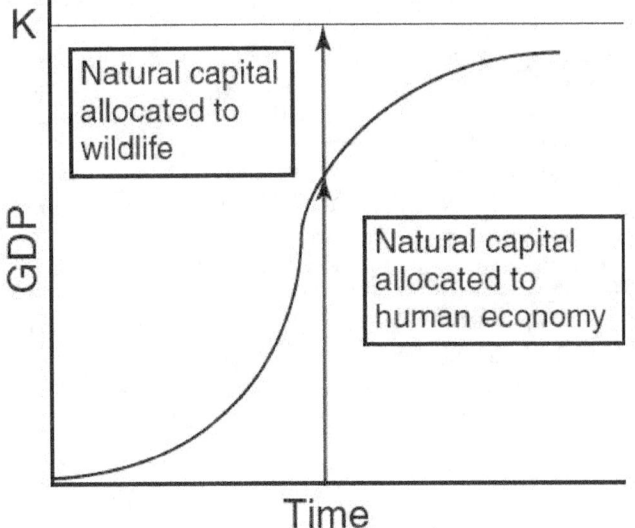

ECONOMIC TROPHIC LEVELS

In the economy of nature, most species exist within distinct trophic levels, or positions within a food chain. The producer trophic level consists of plants, which produce food and fiber via the process of photosynthesis for their own survival and reproduction (Begon *et al.* 1996). Primary consumers consume producers, secondary consumers consume primary consumers, tertiary consumers consume secondary consumers, and so on. In general, animals consume organisms residing in one or more lower trophic levels. Few species eat purely animal flesh, but animals that consume substantial quantities of plants in addition to other animals are called omnivores.

Some species such as scavengers, decomposers, and parasites do not readily fit into particular trophic levels. They may be designated as "service providers" in the economy of nature (Daily 1997).

In ecological economics, human economies are seen to follow the same basic rules as the ones governing the economy of nature. Therefore, the human economy also has a trophic structure (Czech 2000b). The "producers" in the human economy are the agricultural and extractive sectors. The "primary consumers" are the heaviest manufacturing sectors such as mineral ore refining. Ever-lighter manufacturing sectors, all the way up to industries such as computer-chip manufacturing, constitute higher level consumers.

As in the economy of nature, various economic actors participate up and down the trophic levels. These "service providers" in the human economy include bankers, janitors, insurance providers, health care providers, waiters, and others.

The most habitat-transforming or habitat-liquidating economic sectors constitute the trophic levels in the human economy while the service sectors are directly analogous to the service providers in the economy of nature.

A rule of thumb in ecology states that the biomass making up a trophic level is approximately 10 percent of the biomass making up the next-lower trophic level (Begon *et al.* 1996). Therefore, plants dominate the economy of nature in terms of biomass, while the "super-carnivores" are relatively rare and have the lowest biomass.

The human economy follows similar rules. Although farming is no longer a dominant occupation, agricultural land (much of which is now corporately owned) still dominates the landscape. Forests and rangelands, where logging and cattle ranching are the most common economic activities, also are prominent features of the landscape. In other words, larger areas are required for the operation of the lower trophic levels in the human economy, as in the economy of nature. The manufacturing and service sectors of the human economy tend to be located in the most economically efficient areas, i.e., in or near urban centers (Hanink 1997).

Urbanization involves the proliferation of light-to-medium manufacturing sectors and service sectors, all supported by the agricultural and extractive sectors operating in rural areas. Largely for the sake of economic efficiency, urban areas also tend to comprise residential areas for the labor force.

NICHE BREADTH, CARRYING CAPACITY, AND COMPETITIVE EXCLUSION

Beginning with the assumption that the human economy is a subset of the ecosystem, the principles most relevant to conservation land acquisition that merge conservation biology with ecological economics are niche breadth, carrying capacity, and competitive exclusion. The principle of competitive exclusion is that no species succeeds except at the expense of other species (Pianka 1974). The underlying assumption is that each species has a carrying capacity, and therefore, the collective set of species has an aggregate carrying capacity. No species can claim a larger share of aggregate carrying capacity without infringing upon the niches and therefore carrying capacities of other species.

In the neoclassical economic growth model, carrying capacity for the human economy is not required (Jones 1998) nor is there an requirement for aggregate carrying capacity. The resulting policy implications are perhaps the most alarming aspect of neoclassical economic growth theory and hint at the ecological shortcomings of neoclassical economics (Hall et al. 2000). The neoclassical growth theory of unlimited potential is mathematically equivalent to the belief that a limited, stationary scale of human economy could be compacted into a perpetually smaller land mass. Neoclassical growth theory violates well-established principles of conservation biology, thus the need for an *ecologically* macroeconomic approach to conservation land acquisition (Czech 2002).

None of this implies that aggregate carrying capacity is static. Aggregate carrying capacity varies with astrophysical, geological, and evolutionary processes (Fortey 1998). For example, aggregate carrying capacity (for life as we know it) on a hypothetical planet with a temperature of absolute zero will increase as temperatures warm due to astrogeological events, but it will decrease beyond a certain temperature and disappear at a prohibitively hot temperature. Meanwhile, species evolve niches that help to alleviate competitive pressures (Begon et al. 1996), thereby increasing aggregate carrying capacity. Even then, an ultimate or final aggregate carrying capacity is entailed by the first and second laws of thermodynamics (Georgescu-Roegen 1971). What is immediately relevant to conservation land acquisition, however, is that when a species succeeds in an unprecedented manner, at a much faster rate than can be explained by astrophysical, geological, and evolutionary processes, the principle of competitive exclusion is fully engaged. The implication is that, due to the tremendous breadth of the human niche and the technologically boosted rate of its expansion, the scale of the human economy increases at the competitive exclusion of wildlife in the aggregate (Czech et al. 2000). Evidence for this relationship is both theoretical and empirical (Trauger et al. 2003). This relationship is, in fact, the reason why conservation lands have become necessary. As with most conservation tools, and by the definition of conservation, a system of conservation lands ultimately amounts to a brake on economic growth.

ASSOCIATION OF URBANIZATION WITH OTHER CAUSES OF SPECIES ENDANGERMENT

Urbanization has led to the imperilment of at least 275 threatened and endangered species in the United States and Puerto Rico (Czech et al. 2000). Urbanization is strongly associated with other prominent causes of endangerment such as roads and industrial development (Czech et al. 2000). This association helps to identify urbanization as both a proximate cause of species endangerment and a co-symptom of the ultimate cause, i.e., economic growth, which results in a higher extent and intensity of urbanization in addition to the various other habitat-transforming economic sectors more common to exurban areas.

ECONOMIC GEOGRAPHY AND LAND PRICES

With economic growth as a national goal and facilitated by a capitalist democracy in which the majority are fully supportive, the scale of the American economy is expanding and will continue to do so for the foreseeable future. This economic expansion has quantitative and qualitative effects on land use. One of the quantitative effects is rising land prices. This rise occurs because all economic sectors rely to some extent directly on a land base from which to conduct activities; farms, factories, and Internet work stations all use space. The productive or agro-extractive trophic level is most land-intensive in terms of acreage required per monetary unit of transaction (Cramer and Jensen 1994). Land prices rise as the scale of the economy expands because (1) the Earth provides a finite land base and therefore land scarcity increases as more land is claimed for economic production; (2) demand for land increases with economic growth due to the trophic structure of human economy, and; (3) prices rise with scarcity and demand (Dobson et al. 1995).

Land prices do not rise uniformly nationwide, however. They rise fastest in areas where the combination of scarcity and demand rises fastest. Land scarcity is a function of economic activity and is most pronounced where lands are already fully employed for economic activity, but in some cases land scarcity results from ecological processes (e.g., desertification). Demand for land may be for production or consumption.

A growing economy, especially a relatively self-sufficient economy such as that of the United States, represents an integrated expansion of its trophic structure (Boulding 1993). It must first have an adequate productive level: farming, mining, logging, ranching, and fishing. The surplus arising from this productive or agro-extractive level enables the division of labor and resulting manufacturing sectors such as those that produce farm implements and extractive equipment. Next, transportation, financial, and information services proliferate. Value is added to products along each step of the way. For example, the value of a unit of iron increases when manufactured into an implement and increases further still when displayed by a retailer at the appropriate marketplace.

The addition of value associated with the trophic structure of the human economy corresponds with a per acre intensification of economic activity. It may take an acre to produce the iron, a quarter of an acre to convert the iron into an implement, and a hundredth of an acre to display it in the marketplace. Because of the simultaneous value-adding and spatial compaction of economic activity, price per acre rises through the trophic levels of the human economy. This helps explain why land prices increase from agro-extractive to manufacturing to servicing properties. It also helps to explain why the destruction of wildlife habitats tends to become more complete proceeding from farm fields to metropolitan centers. As the intensity of economic activity increases, so does competitive exclusion (Czech *et al.* 2000).

Meanwhile, the higher trophic levels tend to conglomerate and eventually make up urban areas due to the efficiencies offered by urbanization. Indeed, this is the economic explanation for urbanization (Monkkonen 1988). When agro-extractive surplus (and therefore relative non-scarcity of agro-extractive land) exists, as it has throughout all major periods of American history, hands are freed for the division of labor, demand for urban properties is highest, and urban land prices are highest. Simultaneously, because of the intensified competitive exclusion occurring in urban areas, urban areas tend to support the least biodiversity.

IMPLICATIONS FOR BIODIVERSITY CONSERVATION VIA LAND ACQUISITION AND PROTECTION

The immediate implications of urbanization and relative land prices to a conservation land acquisition strategy are straightforward: conservation lands are generally most expensive in urban areas, least expensive in rural areas, and intermediate at the interface where manufacturing tends to dominate. Exceptions tend to be associated with consumption-based demand. For example, during periods of economic expansion supporting many wealthy individuals, demand for rural properties with outstanding aesthetic characteristics increases. Prices for these "amenity" properties increase accordingly. Nonetheless, while land prices in these areas may be higher than those of nearby agro-extractive lands, they are seldom as high as commercial urban land prices.

Some of the highest land prices are in areas where production and consumption are both intense, whether urban or rural. For example, downtown casinos and beachfront resorts are extremely valuable properties, especially during economic booms when demand for luxury services remains high (Frank 1999).

In general, however, the positive relationship of economic activity and land prices means that, with a limited acquisition budget, more land may be acquired by focusing on rural areas. This is not the same as saying that the conservation value of rural acquisitions is higher than the conservation value of urban acquisitions, but it is one piece of a puzzle pointing in that direction.

The *long-term* implications of urbanization and relative land prices are not so simple and must take into account the political economy of the United States and economic globalization. In a society with a national goal of economic growth and the proven means (including relative self-sufficiency and international trade

advantages) to pursue that goal, one of the implications is that more land will go into economic production. History also has shown that the ratio of rural to urban land will continue to decline as agriculture becomes more efficient (Cramer and Jensen 1994). This history may ultimately be threatened by declining agricultural productivity due to erosion and other factors, but to the extent that it continues, an increasing proportion of land will be urban (Czech and Krausman 2001). Furthermore, as the United States depends increasingly on raw materials from other nations, as with timber and several mineral resources, much of the national economy and landscape could become dominated by manufacturing and services in urban areas. Areas of the world where this process is further along include Japan and Hong Kong. The relationship between urbanization and species endangerment indicates that, as urban areas proliferate, so will species endangerment. The proliferation of species endangerment will be exacerbated by the increasing fragmentation of habitats by the urban areas themselves and by loss of the connecting infrastructure (Noss and Csuti 1994).

Any potential land acquisition may be considered to fall on a spectrum of economic structure from totally undeveloped (e.g., pristine wilderness) to totally developed (e.g., urban core). At this stage of the nation's development, neither extreme is likely to be considered for conservation acquisition, because wilderness tends to already be protected and urban cores tend not to have the ecological integrity sought after for the sake of biodiversity conservation. Nevertheless, a long portion of the spectrum is relevant. For example, one may compare the acquisition of a ranch in northern-central Montana (relatively wild) with the acquisition of a beachfront property in southeast Florida (relatively urbanized).

When considering the level of economic activity in developing a conservation land acquisition strategy, it is logical that one end of the development spectrum, or perhaps an area somewhere along the spectrum, may be identified that maximizes the conservation value of acquisitions. Selecting lands along the entire spectrum would be nonstrategic unless there was no known or detectable relationship between stage of development and conservation value. The logical starting point, therefore, is to consider each end of the spectrum in terms of relative conservation value.

A conservation land acquisition strategy that prioritizes-intentionally or unintentionally-lands in heavily developed, urbanized areas will result in the acquisition of high-priced lands where species are becoming endangered. This could be a prudent strategy in the context of a *stable* economy. While costs would be high, so would benefits; viz., conservation of endangered species. Indeed, the high conservation value of the parcels in question is why many conservation land acquisitions in recent years have been made in and near urban areas such as Austin (Texas), San Diego (California), and Key West (Florida). However, there is no indication that the implications of a *growing* economy have been considered. Based on the preceding discussion of conservation biology, ecological economics, and economic geography, in a growing economy: (1) the land area harboring endangered species will increase at an increasing rate as fragmentation, human disturbance, pollution, and other threats associated with urbanization proliferate; (2) land prices will increase most rapidly precisely where species become endangered most rapidly; (3) the areas where the highest prices are paid will be the same areas where species survival is least likely, and (4) higher operating costs associated with intensive user demands, law enforcement, and boundary maintenance in urban areas will reduce the long-term conservation value of urban acquisitions.

In the context of economic growth, the prudence of a strategy that prioritizes lands in relatively undeveloped, rural areas is indicated by the following characteristics: (1) while fragmentation, human disturbance, pollution, and other threats proliferate, rural areas will generally be affected last and least; (2) land prices will increase least rapidly where species become endangered least rapidly; (3) the areas where the lowest prices will be paid will be the same areas where species survival is most likely; and (4) lower operating costs in rural areas will tend to increase the long-term conservation value of rural acquisitions.

Even in a stable economy, an argument could be made for the prudence of prioritizing rural lands. While benefits related to biodiversity conservation might be lower per unit area, so would costs, resulting in a larger addition of conservation lands per funding cycle and, perhaps, greater overall biodiversity conservation. Theoretically, however, these conservation lands would not be required in a stable economy because a stable economy would not require an expanding land base for economic production and consumption. In other words, the rural lands would not be subject to a higher level of competitive exclusion than that already operating. Acquisition of high-priced lands instead would have the simple effect of re-situating economic activities away from urban areas, but only to the extent required by the scale of the stable economy. Perhaps the strongest case that could be made for prioritizing rural lands in the context of a stable economy would be as an "insurance policy" for a potential shift in national policy or performance from economic stability to economic growth.

The prudence of prioritizing rural lands for acquisition in a stable economy is like theoretical icing on an empirical cake, however, because the United States is not poised for economic stabilization. While today's economy consists of some rapidly developing areas where species endangerment is rampant, in a growing economy all areas not set aside for conservation will eventually be developed and the list of endangered or otherwise imperiled species will grow. The implication is that the acquisition of as much area as possible, as soon as possible, will minimize species endangerment in the long run.

Based on the comparison thus far, and in the context of economic growth, the more appropriate conservation land acquisition strategy would prioritize lands in undeveloped, rural areas. What has not been considered, however, is the relationship of biodiversity to land prices. Some of the most expensive areas, such as estuarine shorelines along the Gulf of Mexico, are "biodiversity hotspots" (Dobson et al. 1997). Meanwhile, less expensive areas, such as lodgepole pine forests in the northern Rockies, often support relatively little biodiversity. Unfortunately, the relationship of biodiversity to land prices is far from straightforward, as the history of wetlands development exemplifies. Wetland

prices were very low for most of American history until the technology became available to develop them and the marginal benefits of drainage gradually exceeded the marginal costs (Vileisis 1997). These wetlands were rich in biodiversity while land prices were low, but became low in biodiversity as development proceeded and land prices increased. For example, some of the most expensive real estate in the United States may be found in Washington, DC, which was once a vast wetland and now contains scant ecological integrity (including native biodiversity).

Furthermore, biodiversity hotspots have typically been identified based upon numbers of species (Dobson et al. 1997), which are not equal representatives of biodiversity. Functional genome size, phylogenetic distinctiveness, and molecular clock speed should all be considered in prioritizing species for conservation (Czech and Krausman 1998). Based on these properties, one may argue that it is more important to conserve a large-bodied species (e.g, grizzly bear) by conserving lodgepole pine and other habitats than it is to conserve several small-bodied species by conserving a particular estuarine habitat.

This brief consideration of the relationship of biodiversity to land prices is sufficient to demonstrate that it is much more difficult to quantify conservation benefits than it is to quantify costs-particularly the monetary component of costs. The criteria for assessing the conservation benefits of a parcel are beyond the scope of this paper. Clearly, however, there is a relationship between the conservation value of a land acquisition and the cost of the acquisition, with lower price per acre generally associated with higher conservation value.

CONCLUSION

Economic growth proceeds at the competitive exclusion of biodiversity, including nonhuman species in the aggregate. Principles of economic geography indicate that urbanization will continue as a function of economic growth, while principles of conservation biology indicate that the most thorough competitive exclusion occurs in urban areas. The synthesis of these findings is that urbanization is somewhat of a red herring in the greater debate of economic growth vs. biodiversity conservation. Microeconomic and microecological approaches to biodiversity conservation in and around urban areas may be taken, but the results should be viewed as short-term compromises and perhaps an inefficient use of scarce conservation resources. As long as economic growth remains a primary policy goal, and to the extent such policy is effective, urbanization and biodiversity loss will continue. The only long-lasting approach to biodiversity conservation appears to be macroeconomic: i.e., the establishment of a steady state economy.

LITERATURE CITED

Begon, M.; Harper, J.L.; Townsend, C.R. 1996. Ecology: individuals, populations and communities. 3rd ed. Oxford, UK: Blackwell Science. 1,068 p.

Boulding, K.E. 1993. The structure of a modern economy: the United States, 1929-89. Washington Square, NY: New York University Press. 215 p.

Cramer, G.L.; Jensen, C.W. 1994. Agricultural economics and agribusiness. 6th ed. New York, NY: John Wiley and Sons. 534 p.

Czech, B. 2000a. Economic growth as the limiting factor for wildlife conservation. Wildlife Society Bulletin. 28(1): 4-14.

Czech, B. 2000b. Shoveling fuel for a runaway train: errant economists, shameful spenders, and a plan to stop them all. Berkeley, CA: University of California Press. 216 p.

Czech, B. 2002. A transdisciplinary approach to conservation land acquisition. Conservation Biology. 16(6): 1488-1497.

Czech, B.; Krausman, P.R. 1998. The species concept, species prioritization, and the technical legitimacy of the Endangered Species Act. North American Wildlife and Natural Resources Conference Transactions. 62: 514-524.

Czech, B.; Krausman, P.R. 2001. The Endangered Species Act: history, conservation biology, and public policy. Baltimore, MD: Johns Hopkins University Press. 212 p.

Czech, B.; Krausman, P.R.; Devers, P.K. 2000. Economic associations among causes of species endangerment in the United States. Bioscience. 50(7): 593-601.

Daly, H.E. 1996. Beyond growth: the economics of sustainable development. Boston, MA: Beacon Press. 264 p.

Daily, G., ed. 1997. Nature's services: societal dependence on natural ecosystems. Washington, DC: Island Press. 392 p.

Dobson, A.P.; Rodriquez, J.P.; Roberts, W.M.; Wilcove, D.S. 1997. Geographic distribution of endangered species in the United States. Science. 275: 550-553.

Dobson, S.; Maddala, G.S.; Miller, E.M. 1995. Microeconomics. New York, NY: McGraw-Hill. 378 p.

Fortey, R. 1998. Life: a natural history of the first four billion years of life on Earth. New York, NY: Alfred A. Knopf. 346 p.

Frank, R. H. 1999. Luxury fever: why money fails to satisfy in an era of excess. New York, NY: Free Press. 326 p.

Georgescu-Roegen, N. 1971. The entropy law and the economic process. Cambridge, MA: Harvard University Press. 457 p.

Hall, C.A.S.; Jones, P.W.; Donovan, T.M.; Gibbs, J.P. 2000. The implications of mainstream economics for wildlife conservation. Wildlife Society Bulletin. 28(1): 16-25.

Hanink, D.M. 1997. Principles and applications of economic geography: economy, policy, environment. New York, NY: John Wiley and Sons. 512 p.

Jones, C.I. 1998. Introduction to economic growth. New York, NY: W. W. Norton. 200 p.

Monkkonen, E. H. 1988. America becomes urban: the development of U.S. cities and towns 1780-1980. Berkeley, CA: University of California Press. 332 p.

Noss, R.F.; Csuti, B. 1994. Habitat fragmentation. In: Meffe, G.K.; Carroll, C.R., eds. Principles of conservation biology. Sunderland, MA: Sinauer Associates: 237-264.

Pianka, E.R. 1974. Evolutionary ecology. New York, NY: Harper and Row. 356 p.

Trauger, D.L.; Czech, B.; Erickson, J.D. et al. 2003. The relationship of economic growth to wildlife conservation. Wildlife Society Technical Review 03-1. Bethesda, MD: The Wildlife Society. 22 p.

Vileisis, A. 1997. Discovering the unknown landscape: a history of America's wetlands. Washington, DC: Island Press. 433 p.

PROTECTING OPEN SPACE IN AND AROUND THE TWIN CITIES METROPOLITAN AREA

Roderick H. Squires[1]

ABSTRACT—There are many efforts to preserve open space from urban development in and around the Twin Cities Metropolitan Area. Some involve public acquisition of a landowner's use rights, either acquiring fee title or encumbering the land with an easement, while others involve public restriction on how a landowner may exercise the use rights. This paper asks, "How should we think of these efforts–in terms of our democratic institutions and in terms of past and future urban growth?"

Approximately 75 percent of the seven-county Twin Cities Metropolitan Area in Minnesota, almost 1.5 million acres, consists of open space, areas without structures typically associated with urbanized land uses (table 1) Some of this open space is composed of tracts of publicly owned land set aside for recreation within the urbanized area. This open space is clearly a specific land use type, even though outdoor recreation includes opportunities for a wide range of activities and thus encompasses a suite of structures. The bulk of the open space, 1.1 million acres, defies any such easy categorization, however. It is "nonurbanized land," publicly and privately owned tracts on the edges of the urbanized areas and adjacent to major transportation corridors. This land is currently being used in a variety of ways, particularly–although by no means exclusively–for agriculture. Paradoxically, in a metropolitan

Table 1.—Land use in the Twin Cities Metropolitan Area (Source: http://www.metrocouncil.org/ metroarea/LandUse/metro%20area.pdf).

Urbanized	Acres	% Surface
Residential	368,610	20.3
Commercial	32,273	1.7
Industrial	56,242	2.9
Highways	25,458	1.3
Open Water	123,971	6.5
Outdoor Recreation	163,286	8.6
Institutional	32,548	1.7
Total	802,388	43

Nonurbanized	Acres	% Surface
Wetlands	169,285	8.9
Undeveloped	355,503	18.7
Agriculture	576,964	30.3
Total	1,101,752	57
Total Area	1,904,140	100

area with abundant open space, the debate about its future is intense, largely because the open space on the edges of the urban area is regarded as space available for future urban purposes and its protection is seen as a way of preventing urban sprawl. The contentious debate about the future of open space in this urban area must be informed by an appropriate geographical and historical framework, and this is what this paper attempts to do.

Open space in the Twin Cities Metropolitan Area reflects the cumulated decisions made by chains of landowners, governments, corporations, and individuals, over a long time to exercise their real property rights–and so use the land surface–in ways that either produced, or at least did not destroy, open space. They have done so in response to public policies made by multiple jurisdictions (fig. 1). Existing jurisdictions consist of the federal government, the state government, the Metropolitan Council (the regional planning agency), 7 counties, 138 cities, and 50 townships. The number of jurisdictions has changed through time. Some of them, such as counties and townships, have a long history; some–the Metropolitan Council and a number of cities for example–have shorter histories. All the jurisdictions, except some of the townships have Web sites where their activities are described (http://www.state.mn.us/).

Open space, then, is a political statement that represents both the cumulated outcomes of the continuous, often acrimonious, debates about the utility of open space and the role and responsibility of government to produce it, and the cumulated response of myriad landowners to public policies embodying the outcomes of those debates. These policies are characterized by legislation, attendant regulation, and subsequent judicial opinions (fig. 2). Open space in the future will similarly reflect public policies and the response of landowners.

Landowners operate in a geographical framework that is relatively clearly defined by the boundaries of the real property they own and that occupy unique locations sited within multiple jurisdictions. Therefore, the responses of landowners to policy can be easily mapped, and the geographical framework of public policies is quite clear. Of course, the number of landowners and the size of the tracts have changed over time,

[1] Department of Geography, University of Minnesota, 414 Social Science Building, Minneapolis MN 55455; e-mail: squires@umn.edu

Citation for proceedings: Bengston, David N., tech. ed. 2005. Policies for managing urban growth and landscape change: a key to conservation in the 21st Century. Gen. Tech. Rep. NC-265. St. Paul, MN: U.S. Department of Agriculture, Forest Service, North Central Research Station. 51 p.

Figure 1.—Jurisdictions in the Twin Cities Metropolitan Area.

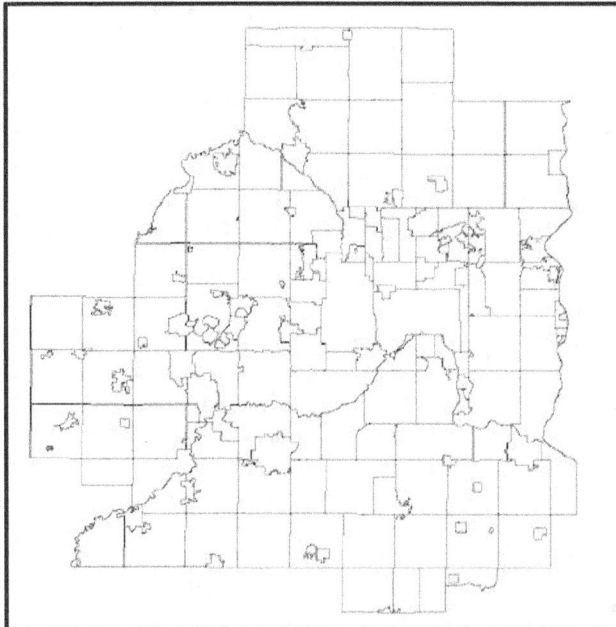

as fragmentation of the land surface and agglomeration–the reverse of fragmentation–have occurred. The present open space can be described either from the perspective of the landowner, focusing on the way in which a particular landowner–a government, a corporation, or a private individual–produces it or from a jurisdictional perspective, focusing on the debates about the utility of open space and the role and responsibility of government in producing it, i.e., the formulation of public policy.

The temporal framework in which landowners operate is not as easily described because the influence of the past is pervasive in so many ways and many landowners continue to use the land as they had in the past. The temporal framework of public policy also is difficult to describe because the debates about the utility of open space and the role and responsibility

Figure 2.—The public policy process.

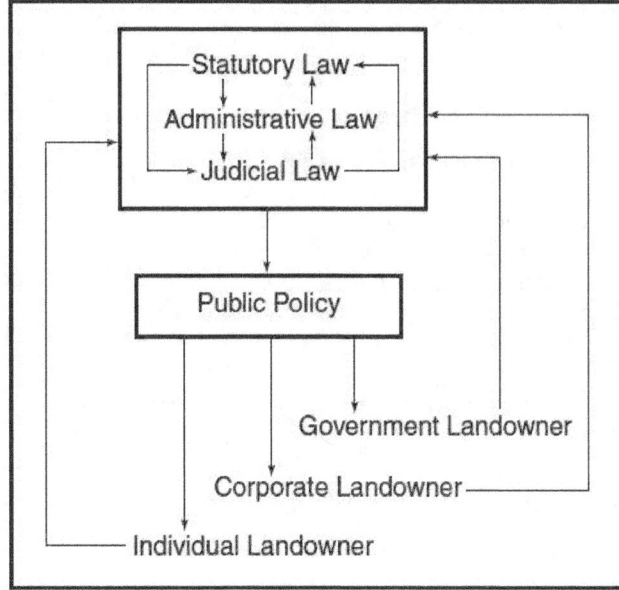

of government to produce it are ongoing. In fact, the role and responsibility each government assumes in producing open space is partly determined by the role and responsibility it inherits from the past and partly by the debates about its present and future roles and responsibilities. If there is not such historic continuity, open space can only be described as a series of historical accidents rather than the cumulated responses of successive landowners to successive public policies designed to produce open space and a particular response of the present landowner to those policies. It is sufficient to assert here that historical continuity and historical inertia are important determinants in describing both current public policies toward open space and landowners' response to those policies.

The amount and distribution of open space have changed over time as governments have recognized the utility of open space, accepted the responsibility for producing it, and established procedures for doing so. At times governments have vigorously promoted such policies and at times they have not. Over time public policies have incorporated more knowledge about the utility of open space and the land use activities that can modify or destroy the ecological characteristics of such areas, about the different methods for producing open space, and about the ways to evaluate the success of such policies. Simply put, the current open space has been produced by a variety of landowners, for a variety of purposes, in a variety of ways, in response to various public policies, and over a long time.

The production of open space in the future will involve the same debates about the utility of open space and the role and responsibility of governments in producing it. In the built-up area the debates will continue a longstanding discussion about the responsibility of governments to provide outdoor recreation opportunities to residents. On the margins of the built-up area, however, the debate will concern the responsibility of governments to produce open space in the face of increased population and the attendant responsibility of government to produce urban uses of the land rather than open space. In both urbanized and nonurbanized areas, existing open space will be preserved only if public policies exist under which particular landowners decide to exercise their real property rights in ways that maintain open space. New open space will be produced only if public policies exist under which particular landowners decide to exercise their real property rights in ways that produce open space.

A PARADIGM FOR OPEN SPACE

In the Twin Cities Metropolitan Area, multiple jurisdictions possess the legal authority over land use activities, and each establishes public policy that contributes to the geographical framework in which particular landowners decide to produce, maintain, or even destroy open space. Some–the federal government, the state government, and the Metropolitan Council–establish policies that influence all landowners living in the metropolitan area. The Metropolitan Council (http://www.metrocouncil.org/) has been given the responsibility for coordinating the land use plans of local governments as well as for planning urban growth. Local governments–counties, municipalities, and townships–establish policies that influence landowners in a smaller geographic area and in a more limited way. Each landowner responds to these multiple public policies by using his/her tracts of land to produce open space or to produce something else that, in effect, destroys open space.

All policy promoting the production of open space, whether such open space is designed to create recreational opportunities or to curb urban sprawl, reflects acceptance that open space is useful and government has a responsibility for producing it. All such policy involves two pathways of production: through public production or through private production (fig. 3)

Governments can produce open space by acquiring fee title to land from private landowners and designating it as open space. Most of the open space that provides opportunities for outdoor recreation within the built-up area is publicly owned and reflects this policy pathway. There is also publicly owned open space in the nonurban area, of which some is set aside specifically for recreation and some is set aside for other reasons, such as wildlife protection. All these lands have been acquired by the government in a variety of ways, by purchasing title from willing sellers, by exchanging land with landowners, by accepting donations of land from individuals, and even by condemning land (fig. 4).

Governments can produce open space by coercing private landowners into producing it. Open space on the margins of the built-up area is largely privately owned, and its production has been elicited in a variety of ways as governments have been extremely inventive and resourceful (fig. 4). Three categories of coercive mechanisms exist. One of these, regulation, is defined by the police power of governments. The other two are defined by the taxing and spending power of governments,

one involving monetary compensation to the affected landowners and the other involving the construction of public works that form part of the urban infrastructure (e.g., transportation lines, sewer and water lines, schools, and libraries). All these forms of coercion have been used in the past to produce open space and are thus embodied in existing public policies and, presumably, will be used in the future.[2]

Regulation

Governments prohibit landowners from exercising their real property rights in ways that would destroy the open space characteristics of their land. This "big stick" approach to producing open space is the oldest and possibly the most contentious coercive tool governments possess. Regulation can either be very specific, targeting landowners who possess real property with valuable ecological characteristics, such as wetlands, blufflands, or floodplains, or it can be very general, operating through zoning ordinances as part of the comprehensive land use planning efforts of governments. Obviously there has to be public will for regulating the activities of particular landowners, but there is a limit to what regulation can occur without it being considered excessive and triggering a "taking" challenge in court.[3] In addition, although the land remains private, its value may be diminished by the regulation and thus affect the tax base of local units of government.

Monetary Compensation

Governments give monetary compensation to specific landowners for not exercising their real property rights in ways that destroy the open space characteristics of their land. This "carrot" approach to producing open space involves a range of compensatory devices. Landowners

Figure 3.—A public/private production spectrum.

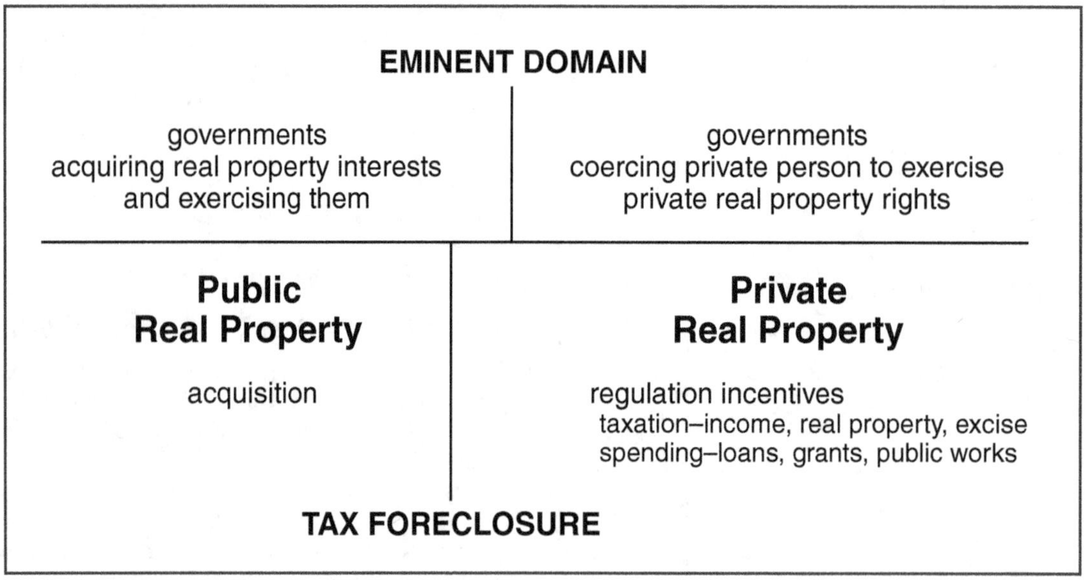

EMINENT DOMAIN	
governments acquiring real property interests and exercising them	governments coercing private person to exercise private real property rights
Public Real Property	**Private Real Property**
acquisition	regulation incentives taxation–income, real property, excise spending–loans, grants, public works
TAX FORECLOSURE	

---

[2] All have a history of use by particular governments. An examination of the utility of these methods in open space production cycles would be interesting and informative but is beyond the scope of the paper.

[3] The line between private and public lands is defined by the point at which courts have decided that government regulation has denied a landowner all reasonable use of the land and thus moves along the public-private spectrum.

Figure 4.—Tools for producing open space.

Promoting transfer of real property rights to "conservation" owner or public	Coercing existing landowner to exercise real property rights in a particular way
Sale of fee title	Management agreement
Sale of fee with reservation of life estate	Registry program
Donation of fee title	Stewardship program
Donation of fee with life estate	Land retirement program
Donation of fee by bequest	Restoration (cost-share) program
Sale/donation of fee with deed restriction	Property tax relief program
Donating conservation easement	Zoning
Selling conservation easement	Subdivision regulation
Mutual covenant	Constructing transportation links
Lease	
Bargain sale	
Exchange	
Condemnation	

receive grants, which they do not repay, loans, which are repaid often at very favorable interest; and many tax breaks—on income, on purchased goods and capital expenditures, and on real property. Obviously, the public has to support providing such compensation, but governments generally appear to have an insatiable appetite for them, especially tax breaks that encourage preferred behavior and, by exclusion, deter undesirable behavior.

Urban Infrastructure

Governments construct the roads and other public works, such as water and sewer lines, that are deemed necessary for providing urban services to existing landowners and for directing urban growth. These public services stimulate the growth of private services such as solid waste disposal, and electrical, gas, and telephone services. The provision of wastewater treatment services in the Metropolitan Urban Services Area is, in fact, a prime tool of the Metropolitan Council in directing urban growth in the Twin Cities Metropolitan Area (Johnson 1998).[4] But the regional transportation network also is a big factor in urban growth.

The Conservation Easement

Conservation easements have become popular in the past decade throughout the nation (Gutanski and Squires 2000). They combine elements of both pathways of open space production described above. Owners of land with open space characteristics voluntarily convey some of their rights to use the land surface to public agencies or to certain nonprofit corporations and receive monetary compensation in the form of income tax and property tax relief. The land burdened by conservation easements remains privately owned but may be open to the public.

Costs and Benefits of the Tools Used to Produce Open Space

All methods of producing open space have costs and benefits, both known and unknown. All are dependent on the debates about the utility of open space, the role and responsibility of government to produce it, the subsequent public policies that emerge, and the response of landowners to those policies. Governments can acquire land to produce open space only (a) if they accept responsibility for producing open space by doing so, rather than leaving such land in private ownership, (b) if they are willing and able to appropriate funds in order to acquire and manage the land, (c) if owners of land with particular ecological characteristics are willing to convey title to the government, and (d) if both governments and landowners are willing to have the land removed from the property tax roles. This strategy requires funds to acquire the land parcels and to maintain their ecological characteristics and so may not be possible in times of restricted government finances. The greatest objection to this approach, however, is that the land is removed from the property tax rolls and is not popular with local governments relying on the property tax as their principal source of revenue. In times of limited budgets and diminished political will, this approach is not possible.

Governments can coerce private landowners into producing open space only (a) if they accept responsibility for producing open space by doing so, (b) if they are willing and able to establish adequate regulatory or compensatory programs or to construct public works, and (c) if owners of tracts with particular open space ecological characteristics are willing to have their uses restricted in some fashion.

---

[4] The MUSA boundary line is the outer edge of the urban area. It is a line agreed to jointly by the council and local governments through local comprehensive plan reviews. It delimits the outer reaches of regional services for the specified time period. Smaller cities beyond this line have established Local Urban Service Areas (LUSA) that similarly provide wastewater treatment facilities.

AN INVENTORY OF
RECREATIONAL OPEN SPACE

Tracts of land of varying sizes and name, specifically designated for outdoor recreational opportunities, exist throughout the urban and nonurban portions of the Twin Cities Metropolitan Area. Virtually every jurisdiction, in fact, owns and manages recreational open space. Most of this type of open space reflects long-established and well-entrenched public policies under which governments have acquired land and produced outdoor recreation opportunities.

Producing such open space was, and is, relatively simple. Governments identify suitable parcels of land and acquire fee title to them from private owners either voluntarily, by purchasing them, by exchanging them for other lands, or by persuading the owners–often using monetary incentives–to donate the lands to the public. Or, governments can acquire land from private owners involuntarily, by exercising their power of eminent domain. These lands have been acquired over the entire existence of some governments. Some tracts were acquired a long time ago, and their continued existence reflects persistent public policies that value open space and government ownership of it. Some tracts were acquired recently and reflect more recent debates about the utility of open space and the role and responsibility of governments. Many recreation units have grown over time as governments have acquired different parcels in different ways for open space purposes. There is every reason to suppose, given such longstanding commitment to outdoor recreation by jurisdictions in the metropolitan area, that in the future the existing open space will be maintained and additional recreational open space will be produced. There will, of course, be periods when public policy in a particular jurisdiction allows government to acquire fee title to land with the specific ecological characteristics. There will also be periods when public policy does not allow such acquisitions, because land is not available at an appropriate price, for example. What follows is an overview of the range of recreational open space areas that exist in the Twin Cities Metropolitan Area.

Federal Government

The National Park Service manages two units in the metropolitan area, the St. Croix National Scenic Riverway (http://www.nps.gov/sacn/) and the Mississippi National River Recreation Area (http://www.nps.gov/miss/index.htm). The U.S. Fish and Wildlife Service manages the Minnesota Valley National Wildlife Refuge and Recreation Area (http://midwest.fws.gov/MinnesotaValley/), the Upper Mississippi Valley Fish and Wildlife Refuge, and various wildlife management areas. These units were established for different purposes at different times, and lands within their boundaries were acquired by the federal government in different ways. They include lands owned by the state and local units of government and by corporations and private individuals. The existence of these open spaces relies on government acquisition of real property rights within the boundaries of the units–both fee title and easements–and on the powers of governments to regulate the activities of private landowners that are inholders in the

units. The U.S. Army Corps of Engineers manages three locks and dams and associated recreational areas (http://www.mvp.usace.army.mil/).

State Government

The Minnesota Department of Natural Resources manages several outdoor recreation units in the metropolitan area, including 3 state parks, 3 state trails, 16 scientific and natural areas, and 18 wildlife management areas (http://www.dnr.state.mn.us/index.html). The state provides public access sites to water bodies and fishing piers, and it has established canoe and boating routes throughout the area. All of these, funded in various ways by state appropriations, user fees, and federal money, reflect the state's longstanding commitment to open space. The DNR also promotes a number of programs that reward private landowners for producing open space. The most recent episode in state public policy is one that emphasizes public ownership and quasi public ownership–ownership by nonprofit corporations and local communities–that increasingly necessitates public acquisition of easements rather than fee title.[5]

Local Governments

Each municipality in the metropolitan area provides outdoor recreational opportunities. As early as 1849, private land was donated to the newly established settlement of St. Paul to be used as a park, and 8 years later, lands were donated to Minneapolis for similar use (http://www.minneapolisparks.org/home.asp). The cities continued to acquire and develop park systems throughout the 19th and early 20th centuries. Other local governments also aggressively acquired and developed parkland.

Today, there are 46 parks and park reserves and five special recreation areas–encompassing 47,000 acres–and 22 trails–covering 170 miles–in a regional park system in the metropolitan area. Many of these parks were originally county parks and became regional parks when the Metropolitan Council assumed authority over regional recreational planning (http://www.metrocouncil.org/parks/parks.htm). The council plans this system and makes grants from state appropriations and bond issues to counties, municipalities, and park districts to allow them to buy and manage the land surface according to master plans approved by the council. Each government pays the operation and maintenance costs for the units under its jurisdiction from real property tax revenues, funds from the state legislature, and user fees. Each park district in the metropolitan area has to prepare and submit to the council a master plan and an annual budget to acquire and develop regional open space that is consistent with the council's open space plan.

AN INVENTORY OF THE OPEN SPACE
AT THE URBAN FRINGE

Tracts of nonurbanized open space at the margins of the metropolitan urban area, although not composed of a single land use type, possess two unifying characteristics. The first, rather obviously, is the absence of structures associated with urban land use, apart from a transportation network. The second is

---

[5] See Minnesota DNR (http://www.dnr.state.mn.us/nrplanning/community/index.html) and the McKnight Foundation (http://www.embraceopenspace.org/).

the private ownership of most of the land. The future of these open space tracts in the face of an expanding urban area is engendering much debate. These open spaces will remain only if public policy continues to recognize that such open space possesses utility and governments accept responsibility for producing it, either by acquiring the necessary real property interests in the land or by coercing private landowners into producing it on their own land.

Public policy represents compromise between participants in the debate. It has always embodied multiple, even mutually incompatible, goals. Policy for open space will have to be formulated along with policy for urbanization as population increases in the metropolitan area and as the urbanized area increases. Most obviously, this policy will be reflected in the comprehensive plans developed by local governments and the Metropolitan Council.

Agricultural Land

Approximately 600,000 acres are farmed in the seven-county metropolitan region. These privately owned agricultural lands provide valuable informal outdoor recreational opportunities. Such open space represents the cumulated outcome of public policies in which a succession of private landowners have decided to exercise their real property rights and use the land surface to produce agricultural products and to provide agricultural services, including open space. Maintaining agricultural open space requires federal and state agricultural policies and local comprehensive plans that use a variety of tools to encourage individual farmers to stay in farming rather than to sell their land to developers and move to Florida. Agricultural lands and farmers have long been favored landowners in federal and state policy, and in recent decades governments have developed numerous tools to protect private agricultural lands by providing incentives to the farmland owner to use land in ways that protect farmland—even to the extent of taking land out of production.[6] In addition, governments have provided a variety of disincentives to discourage landowners from engaging in practices that destroy farmland. Such incentives and disincentives underlie policy that tries to coerce farmers into using lands in ways that protect soil, preserve wetlands and wildlife habitat, and avoid contaminating the ground and surface waters with chemicals.

Other Nonurban Land

A variety of land surfaces—wooded, permanently or seasonally wet, or steeply sloping—are "lightly used" because of their ecological characteristics. Some of these lightly used lands have been set aside as public recreation open space, but the majority of them provide valuable informal outdoor recreational opportunities. Maintaining these lands requires public policy that either allows the public to acquire interests in the land or to encourage the owners of these lands to use it in ways that protect its ecological characteristics. Although governments of all types have acquired specific tracts for outdoor recreation purposes, many of the places are maintained by state and local government regulation of landowners' activities.

LOCAL GOVERNMENT INITIATIVES

Increasingly, protecting open space on the urban margins has become a local concern, although not without some conflict between governments.[7] In November 2002 voters in Dakota County authorized the county board to issue bonds worth $20 million to protect farmland and natural resources financed through a 10-year property tax increase. The open spaces considered important to protect—because of their location and their ecological characteristics—have been identified in a Farmland and Natural Area Protection Plan (http://www.co.dakota.mn.us/planning/fnap/Index.htm). Lands are to be protected by using conservation easements to acquire real property interests and limit their use, providing management expertise to landowners, promoting the state Metropolitan Agricultural Preservation Program, and guiding urban development away from these lands through zoning (http://www.revisor.leg.state.mn.us/stats/40A/).

NONPROFIT ORGANIZATIONS

Throughout the United States nonprofit corporations whose sole goal is to preserve the ecological characteristics of certain types of land have emerged to advocate public policies that protect open space and to supplement and complement the efforts of governments in the protection effort. Minnesota has not experienced the tremendous growth in these nonprofit organizations, such as land trusts, that have appeared elsewhere, possibly because of the long-established public policies of governments acquiring land to preserve as open space. A few national organizations, such as The Nature Conservancy and the Land for Public Trust, acquire real property rights they sometimes convey to governments and sometimes maintain possession. The Nature Conservancy recently helped the federal government establish the Glacial Ridge National Wildlife Refuge in Minnesota (http://nature.org/wherewework/northamerica/states/minnesota/), and the Trust for Public Land is active in Minnesota (http://www.tpl.org/). The Izaak Walton League (http://www.mtn.org/~mn-ikes/) and the North Star Chapter of the Sierra Club (http://northstar.sierraclub.org/) also are involved in protecting open space. The Land Trust Alliance keeps track of open space public policy and the efforts of nonprofits throughout the nation (http://www.lta.org/publicpolicy/index.html).

There also are a number of local nonprofits. Some acquire fee title and then transfer ownership to governments, such as the Parks and Trail Council of Minnesota (http://www.parksandtrails.org/). Some acquire title and conservation easements and maintain ownership, such as the Minnesota Land Trust (http://www.mnland.org/). The majority of them, however, lobby governments to formulate policy protecting open space,

---

[6] See the United States Department of Agriculture (http://www.usda.gov/wps/portal/usdahome), the Minnesota Department of Agriculture (http://www.mda.state.mn.us/), the American Farmland Trust (http://www.farmland.org/) and the Farmland Trust Information Center (http://www.farmlandinfo.org/).

[7] For example, in a recent case, *City of Lake Elmo v Metropolitan Council*, the Minnesota Appeals Court upheld the authority of the Metropolitan Council to force the city to change its land use plans and allow more urbanization. See http://www.lawlibrary.state.mn.us/archive/ctappub/0312/opa030458-1216.htm.

usually focusing on government or nonprofit acquisition of real property rights rather than the coercion of private landowners to use land in particular ways. Examples include the Midtown Greenway Coalition (http://www.midtowngreenway.org/), Friends of the Minnesota River Valley (http://www.friendsofmnvalley.org/default.htm), Friends of the Mississippi River (http://www.fmr.org/), Great River Greening (http://www.greatrivergreening.org/), Minnesota Center for Environmental Advocacy (http://www.mncenter.org), and 1,000 Friends of Minnesota (http://www.1000fom.org/).

CONCLUSIONS

The amount and distribution of open space that currently exists in the Twin Cities Metropolitan Area represent the cumulated decisions made by landowners exercising their real property rights in a public policy context reflected in statutory, administrative, and case law.[8] This open space, and the ways in which it is produced, have evolved over the past century. Each parcel of open space possesses a unique history.

How much of this open space will remain depends on whether governments are convinced that open space is useful, if not vital, and that they have a role and responsibility for producing it. Public policy promoting the production of open space will require an electorate, represented by the elected and appointed officials, supporting legislative, executive, and judicial decisions that permit governments either (a) to acquire

the real property interests necessary to ensure the desired open space is maintained, or (b) to coerce open space landowners to use their land in ways that maintain those characteristics through regulation, through various financial incentives and disincentives, and through the construction of road, wastewater facilities, and other public institutions (fig. 5). There is no "silver bullet" for protecting open space in the Twin Cities Metropolitan Area. Increasing population will be accommodated in new urban areas adjacent to existing urban areas and in the redeveloped old urban areas. Inevitably, as the urban area expands, it will both continue to sprawl and, in some places, become denser. New tools will be developed to allow governments to acquire real property interests and to coerce individuals. Innovative financing and legal arrangements will allow communities, rather than governments, to acquire and maintain open space.

LITERATURE CITED

Gutanski, J.A.; Squires, H.R. eds. 2000. Protecting the land: conservation easements past, present, and future. Washington, DC: Island Press. 566 p.

Johnson, W.C. 1998. Growth management in the Twin Cities region: the politics and performance of the Metropolitan Council. Center for Urban and Regional Affairs, Publication No. CURA 98-3. Minneapolis, MN: Hubert H. Humphrey Institute of Public Affairs, University of Minnesota. 111 p.

Figure 5.—A decision-tree for open space.

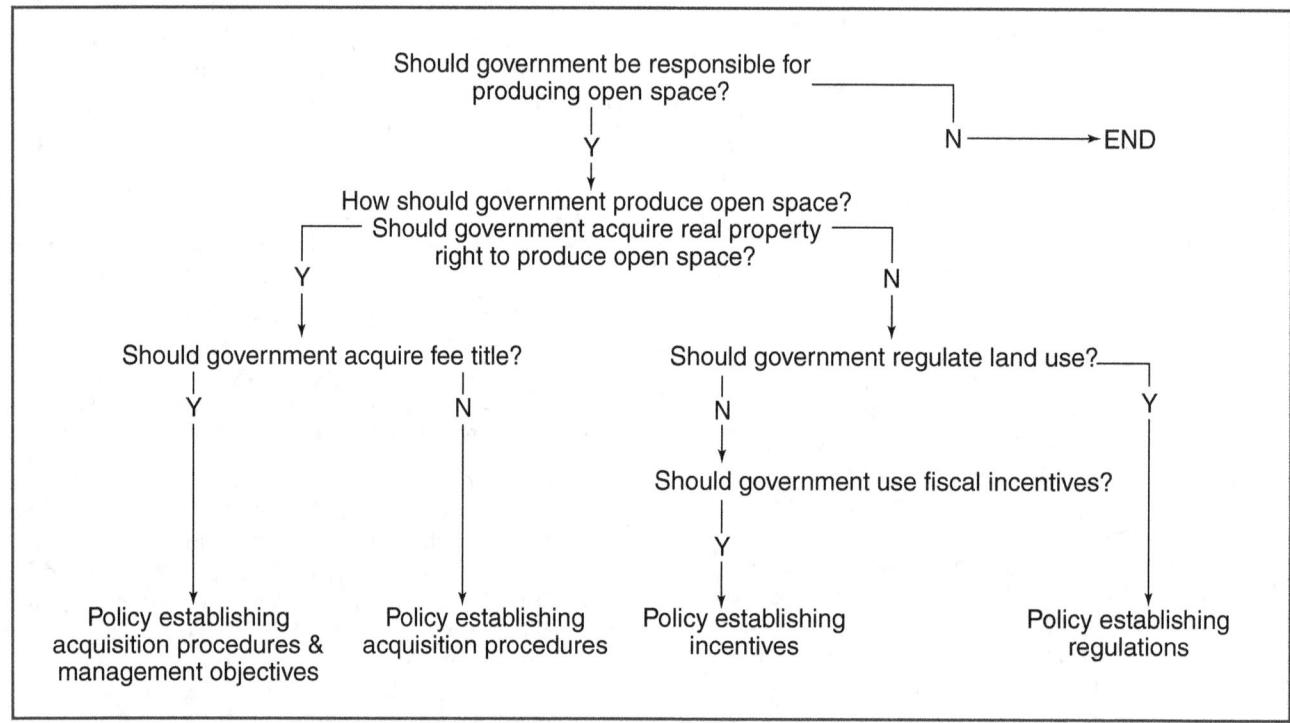

---

[8] Only parts of the public policies that have resulted in the current open space are still represented in current law. Parts of previous policies have been repealed, amended, and superseded over time.

BROWNFIELD REDEVELOPMENT:
A HIDDEN OPPORTUNITY FOR CONSERVATION BIOLOGY

Lynne M.Westphal,[1] Jeffrey M. Levengood,[2] Alaka Wali,[3] David Soucek,[2] Douglas F. Stotz[3]

ABSTRACT—Brownfields—lands that are idle due to concerns about contamination—are often prominent features of urban areas. Conservation in an urbanizing world must take brownfields into consideration because regions of heavy industry can harbor areas of ecological significance. The Calumet region of northwest Indiana and northeast Illinois is one such place, where the Calumet Initiative, a partnership of government, industry, academia, nonprofit groups, and local residents, is working toward economic and ecological sustainability. Here partners have developed a research and action program that integrates social, biological, and physical issues to move toward a sustainable future. We discuss three current research projects: planning that considers biodiversity as well as redevelopment goals, research that investigates the viability of state-threatened and state-endangered species, and a social asset mapping project. Using a marsh in Calumet that hosts a rookery of the state-endangered black-crowned night heron, as well as other species of concern, and that borders a potential superfund site, we will outline this integrated research and action program and its wider application for conservation biology.

Brownfields are "abandoned, idled, or under-used industrial and commercial facilities where expansion or redevelopment is complicated by real or perceived environmental contamination" (Northeast Midwest Institute 2001: 1). There are an estimated 580,000 brownfields nationwide ranging from former gas stations to derelict industrial plants covering hundreds of acres (Deason *et al.* 2001).

It may seem counterintuitive, but industrialized regions, including brownfields, can contain areas of critical wildlife habitat. Many industrial areas are buffered with large amounts of open land, and many are sited along water for transportation, energy, and other reasons. In some cases industry and landfills were relegated to the lands no one wanted—wetlands. In these areas, habitat can be found between the smokestacks and loading docks. As a result, brownfields and industrial areas sometimes harbor surprising species richness and are therefore often critical to conserving biodiversity in an urbanizing world.

The Calumet region is a highly industrialized area replete with brownfields and remnant habitats. It runs along the southwest shore of Lake Michigan, including 10 percent of the City of Chicago, cities and towns in northwest Indiana, and the Indiana Dunes National Lakeshore. Several rivers run through the Calumet region, providing riparian habitat. Steel and other industrial facilities have large buffer tracts of native habitat, some of it high quality. Calumet's extensive wetland systems once contained marsh, fen, swale, and bog; today valuable remnants remain. The Calumet region was and is ecologically complex: dune and swale, northern boreal forest, desert, prairie, and savanna ecosystems overlap

here (U.S. Department of the Interior, National Park Service Midwest Region 1998).

The Calumet region is historically important for both ecology and industry. In 1898 Henry Cowles first outlined the theory of succession in Calumet's Indiana dunes. At the same time, steel and other industries were moving into Calumet. By the 1920s, Calumet was surpassing Pittsburgh in steel production (and remains the largest steel producing region in the United States today). By the end of World War II, the Calumet region was the largest area of heavy industry in the world.

With the 1970s and 1980s came a drastic global restructuring of the steel industry, and mill after mill closed. Other industries felt these economic shifts too, as the region hemorrhaged jobs, and communities and local families faced hard times. More than 40 percent of the jobs in southeast Chicago were lost between 1970 and 1990 (Jones 1998). As a result of this decline in the region's industrial base, thousands of acres of brownfields were created.

The steel industry and other uses dramatically changed the land. Slag, a gravel-like byproduct of steel-making, was used as landfill in Lake Michigan and in wetlands to create "useful" land. Human-made mountains of municipal and industrial landfills now rise from former wetlands. Rivers have been straightened and deepened to support commercial shipping. Railroads and highways crisscross Calumet, connecting the region to the country and the world. Because of this nexus of transportation resources, the Calumet region is the largest intermodal shipping hub in the United States (City of Chicago Department of Planning and Development 2002).

[1] USDA Forest Service North Central Research Station, 1033 University Place, suite 360, Evanston IL 60201-3172; e-mail: lwestphal@fs.fed.us
[2] Illinois Natural History Survey, Champaign, IL.
[3] Field Museum of Natural History, Chicago, IL.

Citation for proceedings: Bengston, David N., tech. ed. 2005. Policies for managing urban growth and landscape change: a key to conservation in the 21st Century. Gen. Tech. Rep. NC-265. St. Paul, MN: U.S. Department of Agriculture, Forest Service, North Central Research Station. 51 p.

Through the region's industrial growth and decline, wildlife and native vegetation persisted. Although many natural areas have been seriously degraded, enough habitat is left to support a variety of species of conservation interest. Outdoor activities have remained popular in Calumet, too. A hunting and fishing hotspot in the late 1800s and early 1900s, today Calumet still provides some of the most accessible hunting and fishing opportunities in Chicago. Bird watchers and wildlife watchers flock to the area to see state-endangered birds like the black-crowned night heron (*Nycticorax nycticorax*) and snowy egret (*Ardea alba*). Anglers come for the bass and pike, and hunters come for the only remaining legal hunting in Chicago. Local residents have been active for decades on behalf of local wildlife and recreation, arguing for protection and enhancement of Calumet's natural riches.

In 2000 the City of Chicago and State of Illinois announced a major initiative to revitalize the economy while also conserving and enhancing the biodiversity of the Illinois part of the Calumet region. The Calumet Initiative, a partnership of government, industry, academia, museums, nonprofit groups, and local residents, is working toward economic and ecological sustainability in Calumet. One key site in the region is Indian Ridge Marsh.

The 145-acre Indian Ridge Marsh, divided by a street into north (110 acres) and south (35 acre) sections, was a beach ridge used for travel first by Native Americans and then by Europeans. By the late 1800s Indian Ridge Marsh was platted for residential development, and a handful of houses were built. Ironically, being platted probably saved Indian Ridge Marsh, because gaining ownership of the land entailed dealing with hundreds of owners of individual plots and the City of Chicago used a process to reclaim tax-delinquent property to purchase most of Indian Ridge Marsh for public ownership. Neighboring sites include a landfill that is a potential superfund site, an active freight rail line, a heavy truck route, and a former steel coke plant. Indian Ridge Marsh is one of the first Calumet sites to move into public ownership with plans for ecological rehabilitation and is the site for several research projects. It is home to numerous species of marsh-dependent breeding birds, including the black-crowned night heron, native vegetation patches (including jewelweed [*Impatiens capensis*] and pale sedge [*Carex granularis*]), and a buried but viable and rich native seed bank. Unfortunately, like many disturbed urban sites, Indian Ridge Marsh also has significant invasive species populations and contamination concerns (including purple loosestrife [*Lythrum salicaria*], phragmities [*Phragmites australis*], DDE, and ammonia).

The black-crowned night heron rookery in Indian Ridge Marsh is one of the two largest remaining heron rookeries in Illinois. Although this species is not threatened nationally or globally, it is a state-endangered species, and this rookery is of great importance for local and regional residents. The number of nests associated with this colony averaged 610 between 1985 and 1993 (S. Elston, USEPA, unpubl. data). More recently, the number of herons comprising this rookery declined from approximately 1,500 adults in 1996 to 559 (approximately 200 nesting pairs) in 2000 (W. Marcisz, pers. comm.), although numbers have been relatively stable since then.

RESEARCH TO SUPPORT CONSERVATION OF CALUMET AREA HABITAT

From population genetics to applied phytoremediation, conservation biology spans a wide continuum of disciplines. Academic exercises and applied research both find a home in this growing discipline. In Calumet, the research program spans this continuum as well, although most research is designed to address specific needs in the Calumet Initiative. That does not, however, preclude work that also addresses theoretical issues in conservation biology, but in the context of Calumet these theoretical issues are folded into research with an applied component as well. In the Calumet region, partners have developed a research and action program that integrates social, biological, and physical issues to move toward a sustainable future. More than two dozen research projects are underway, involving research partners from the Field Museum of Natural History; the Illinois Scientific Surveys (Water, Natural History, Geology, and Waste Management Research Center); the USDA Forest Service, North Central Research Station; and universities. In this section, we will discuss three of the Calumet Initiative research projects, using Indian Ridge Marsh in Calumet as an example. These projects are a planning project that considers biodiversity as well as redevelopment goals, research that investigates the viability of state-endangered species, and social asset mapping to support community goals and facilitate collaboration between local residents and conservation groups.

Planning That Considers Biodiversity as Well as Redevelopment Goals

One of the first steps necessary in the Calumet Initiative was planning, from a regional perspective to site-level designs. The Chicago Department of Planning and Development, in partnership with the Chicago Department of Environment, the Southeast Chicago Development Commission, the Openlands Project, and the Calumet Area Industrial Council, developed the *Calumet Land Use Plan* (City of Chicago Department of Planning and Development 2002). This plan outlines the ideas of ecological and economic growth and redevelopment, designating a significant amount of land for each use. Plans for the natural areas are further outlined in the *Calumet Open Space Reserve Plan* and the *Calumet Area Ecological Management Strategy* (EMS; City of Chicago Department of Environment 2002). Because the EMS addresses ecological rehabilitation priorities and strategies, of the three plans it is most directly related to the goals of conservation biology. The EMS looks in more detail at several sites surrounding Lake Calumet, including Indian Ridge Marsh. The plan was developed with input from more than 160 organizations and individuals who met in theme-based sessions (e.g., vegetation, sediments and toxics, recreation) in which participants outlined what was known about each site, what was not known, and which of these knowledge gaps were most critical. This information was processed and integrated by a 13-member Integration Advisory Team, made up of Calumet Initiative members with diverse specialties including wetland hydrology, ornithology, planning, and recreation.

The EMS planning process resulted in a decisionmaking format called Preserve, Improve, Create, or PIC (figure 1 shows the PIC table for Indian Ridge Marsh). This format allows decisionmakers to quickly identify the most critical attributes at any site to preserve–providing a litmus test for ecological rehabilitation or other site alterations. If there is a significant risk of harm to something on the "preserve" list or a significant gap in our knowledge that makes it impossible to estimate the risk, then the proposed change will not move forward. At Indian Ridge Marsh, the black-crowned night heron rookery is one of the key attributes to preserve. Next, in the second tier of importance,

attributes in need of improvement are identified (including everything that is to be preserved). Finally, the "create" category recognizes areas so degraded that much creativity will be needed to make any headway with ecological rehabilitation. The EMS Integration Advisory Team identified several key knowledge gaps critical to several disciplines; a multisite hydrologic analysis and master plan is one example.

Figure 1.—Preserve, Improve, Create (PIC) Chart for Indian Ridge Marsh. Shading indicates important sites considered in the EMS; a checkmark indicates importance at Indian Ridge Marsh.

Resource Categories	Resource Targets	P Preserve[1]	I Improve	C Create
Wetland Habitat & Wildlife	Marsh habitat	✓		
	• Potential black-crowned night heron habitat	✓		
	• Transitional habitat for birds–includes common reed where it provides critical short-term habitat	✓		
	• Other marsh-dependent breeding birds	✓		
	• Native emergent marsh vegetation	✓		
	• Amphibian habitat (frogs and mud puppies)			
	Existing native seed banks	✓		
	Other habitat critical to species of concern[2]	✓		
	Shorebird habitat			
	Submergent species assemblages			
Upland Habitat & Wildlife	Other habitat critical to species of concern[2]			
	Upland habitat		✓	
	Vegetation quality (Prairie, Woodland)		✓	
	Grassland habitat		✓	✓
	Diverse upland habitat structure (grasslands, brush, small trees, etc.)			✓
	Grassland assemblages of birds and herpetiles			
Aquatic Habitat	Other habitat critical to species of concern[2]			
	Native fish habitat			
Water/Hydrology	Current functional hydrologic connections	✓		
	Other habitat critical to species of concern[2]			
	Water levels (control of fluctuations)		✓	
	Water quality (control of ground water and surface water pollutants)		✓	
Physical Parameters	Native soils	✓		
	Soil quality		✓	
	Sediment quality		✓	
Socioeconomic Parameters	People's attachment to places		✓	
	Regional/interstate access to region		✓	
	Recreational uses that do not conflict with ecological goals or safety concerns	✓		✓
	Opportunities for learning about local nature and native landscapes		✓	

[1] Anything in the "preserve" category will also be "improved."
[2] A critical gap is complete inventories for each site. There may, therefore, be more species of conservative interest on these sites that we do not know about yet.

Nesting Ecology and Contaminant Exposure of the Lake Calumet Black-Crowned Night Heron Colony

With the Calumet region's history of heavy industrial activity, sewage and industrial discharges, landfills, and hazardous waste storage/disposal, sediments here contain elevated concentrations of organic and inorganic contaminants that may pose risks to fish-eating wildlife (Halbrook et al. 1999, Hothem et al. 1995, Ohlendorf et al. 1978, Price 1977). Black-crowned night herons nesting at Indian Ridge Marsh are known to forage throughout the Calumet area, often in areas characterized by elevated concentrations of environmental contaminants. Some of these contaminants may bioaccumulate in the herons via transfer up the aquatic food chain. Herons and egrets have been used extensively as bioindicators/biomonitors of environmental contamination (e.g., Blus et al. 1985, Custer et al. 1997, Fleming et al. 1984, Halbrook et al. 1999). Their trophic position and aquatic foraging habits may put them in contact with prey that accumulate/bioconcentrate high concentrations of environmental contaminants such as organochlorine pesticides, PCBs, and metals found in sediments in the Calumet area. Various effects of exposure to such contaminants have been documented in black-crowned night heron, including eggshell thinning and reduced reproductive success (Price 1977, Ohlendorf et al. 1978, Henny et al. 1984, Findholt and Trost 1985), hatching success (Custer et al. 1983), reduced embryo weights (Hoffman et al. 1986), responses in biochemical markers of exposure (Rattner et al. 1997, 2000), possible teratogenic effects (Hothem et al. 1995), and cytogenetic damage (Custer et al. 1994).

This research examined various aspects of the ecology of the Indian Ridge Marsh heron colony during 2002 and 2003 breeding seasons to provide information that will aid in conserving the colony. To help with remediation and restoration planning, we determined nesting phenology and nest-site characteristics. We also examined whether the colony's herons were being exposed and harmed by elevated concentrations of priority contaminants present in Calumet sediments. This particular study characterizes the foraging habits of the colony as a whole, determines concentrations of priority contaminants in aquatic prey items (fish, crayfish) at selected foraging sites as well as in regurgitated food items collected at nests, and examines markers of reproduction and health.

Our study revealed that young black-crowned night herons at Indian Ridge Marsh are exposed to a number of organic contaminants at concentrations that induce detoxification enzymes. Although we observed normal productivity and early survival, it is impossible to determine how the enzyme induction might affect juveniles after dispersal and during their first migrational movements, a time of physiological stress and high mortality in young birds. We do know that juveniles feed extensively in the natal marsh and that efforts to reduce contaminant inputs will likely reduce the contaminant burden of young herons. The adults forage throughout the south Chicago region, at both highly contaminated and relatively "clean" sites. Thus, efforts to conserve this population extend beyond the nesting marsh.

Management and rehabilitation activities must consider black-crowned night herons nesting behavior. In recent years this colony has nested exclusively in the emergent Phragmities cover; thus rehabilitation efforts need to consider providing alternative vertical structure for nesting if rehabilitation plans call for Phragmities removal. Widely fluctuating water levels due to stormwater inputs threaten the nesting effort in most years, thus there is a need for water control to emulate the natural cycle. The long nesting season, from April (first eggs laid) through August (last young disperse) in this asynchronous breeder, dictates that disruptive construction activities be scheduled early or late in the year.

Social Assets in Calumet–Keys to Conservation

The mapping of "social assets" is a useful way to begin involving local residents in conservation efforts. Drawing on the methodology of Kretzmann and McKnight (1993), the mapping project identified significant organizations, institutions, nodes of informal networks, and other local social resources. It also analyzed local perceptions about the environment and nearby natural habitats. Analysis of these data revealed patterns allowing the significant assets to be layered on a physical map of the region, using Geographic Information Systems software. The result is an accessible representation of the sources of civic activism and the links between different types of activism and concerns for the environment (www.fieldmuseum.org/calumet). This information can be useful in promoting citizen participation in conservation programs as well as in drawing active individuals and organizations into the arena of conservation or environmental restoration.

The neighborhood of South Deering, adjacent to Indian Ridge Marsh, provides a specific example of the application of social asset mapping to conservation biology. This neighborhood, as an officially designated community area, actually encompasses three distinct communities from the perspective of residents: South Deering, Vets Park, and Jeffrey Manor. The demographics of the region have changed significantly over the years, and according to the 2000 census, South Deering now has a largely Latino and African American population. Each community within the larger South Deering area has distinctive assets—for example, block clubs were a major organizational form in Jeffrey Manor. Vets Park has an "improvement association," which successfully won modifications to the Agrifine Company's animal fat processing plant in 1995. South Deering has an empowerment association that collaborates with the community policing efforts and other public safety-oriented activities. These volunteer associations indicate a level of activism in the neighborhoods and can be a point of contact for conservationists wanting to reach out to local communities. There also are several key churches in the three neighborhoods of South Deering. Similar to the local volunteer associations, churches provide focal points for social gatherings and for action on social issues and moral deliberation. Gardens (both public and private) are common throughout and are important to residents in improving their communities. This is a potential bridge for conservationists because gardening skills and interests may be readily translated to ecological rehabilitation volunteer efforts. Each of these social assets—neighborhood volunteer associations, active churches, and public and private gardening—are applicable to conservation in an urban area. They indicate residents' concerns for place and their ability to organize on behalf of their local environments, and they represent opportunities for collaboration with conservation biologists and other environmentalists from outside the community.

DISCUSSION AND CONCLUSION

While the black-crowned night heron is abundant throughout much of its range, this species is important in Calumet for a variety of reasons. First, the black-crowned night heron is not alone in using Indian Ridge Marsh as a breeding and foraging area. Understanding this colony and improving its habitat will quite likely help other marsh-dependent birds such as the snowy egret (*Egretta thula*), common moorehen (*Gallinula chloropus*), and American bittern (*Botaurus lentiginosus*), species of broader conservation interest.

But more to the point of this paper is the important role that the black-crowned night heron plays in the social landscape of Calumet, and the intertwining of social, biological, and physical issues represented by this species' management. The black-crowned night heron has captivated the local and regional communities. It is a rare, and for many an exhilarating, experience in an urban area to witness a large flock of nesting birds at sunset. Residents want to see these birds, to follow their nesting habits. This offers an opportunity to educate people about conserving habitat, including foraging territory as well as nesting areas. Although we have not tested this hypothesis, it is quite possible that these educational opportunities could broaden people's interest in and support for conservation practices, and for species not near home. If this proves true, the conservation efforts aimed at a relatively abundant species could result in support for conserving more endangered species far from urban population centers.

Local residents' interest in this species is reflected in how the black-crowned night heron colony and Calumet's other natural riches serve as a rallying point for organization and action. Much of the conservation efforts going forward now in Calumet would not be happening were it not for the ongoing hard work of local residents on behalf of the many species of animals and plants that survive in the area. In this way, the fascination with the black-crowned night heron has a ripple effect for other local species in need of habitat improvements.

Yet there is a more subtle, perhaps even more important, issue related to the local interest in this black-crowned night heron colony, one less instrumental for conservationists and more important for local well-being. This aspect rests in the potential social-psychological impact of this colony on the local residents. Calumet has an image problem. The remaining industry and waste disposal facilities create smells and haze and other negative impacts on the area. Past industry left behind toxic dumps and literally tons and tons of slag and other fill. Calumet's local reputation has made this an area avoided by most, which may have increased the feeling of isolation of local communities. In short, many local residents feel they are living in a forsaken area, and some perceive disdain and contempt from the broader Chicago metro community. In environmental psychology, researchers have articulated many of the ways in which the environment in which people live impacts their sense of self. As one of the founders of the field, Harold Proshansky, sums it up, "People not only project onto their environment, they introject from it" (Proshansky 1976). *Projecting* onto the environment can be seen in front yards, styles of homes, and other ways in which people express themselves in their environment. *Introjecting* is the reverse—people defining and valuing themselves based on what they see around them. The connection to the rookery is this: the black-crowned night heron colony and the other natural riches can mitigate the negative influences of *introjecting* from the landfills, sludge drying facilities, and industrial waste that is all too common in Calumet. The Field Museum social asset research team discovered that despite the negative associations that residents know come from the contamination of their environment, both newer and older residents found ways to maintain or create positive associations to place. The older residents drew on the historical memories of a rich fabric of social life constructed during the steel mill era, while newer residents were proud of their nascent efforts at economic revitalization and beautification. The growing awareness of Lake Calumet's rich biodiversity and natural habitats is fast becoming part of residents' armor for defending their way of life and for maintaining their communities. In this way, the black-crowned night heron colony can make meaningful contributions to community well-being. And in this way, conservation biology can contribute to species survival *and* human quality of life.

Renewed interest in economic development in Calumet could have been coming at the expense of the remaining natural areas. But, instead, there is a real effort (with some struggle) to coordinate economic development with ecological rehabilitation. This is not unlike getting conservation to work in developing countries by building in economic opportunities for local residents. This brings us to a final point: in Calumet it is obvious that conservation cannot move forward without taking into account the local social landscape. This is equally true, however, in more remote places. It is true for cultural stability period—be it the cultural stability of the southeast side of Chicago or in the mountains of Peru. Field Museum of Natural History researchers have found that incorporating local interests and expertise in conservation projects in Peru is the only way to have a chance for successful conservation. There seems to be little choice because long-term stewardship of the area depends on it. If local people do not feel ownership, then external agents are less and less likely to succeed in achieving sustainability or conserving remaining flora and fauna.

A key finding in the social asset study suggests one reason why this is true, one that is different from the common wisdom of the need to honor the livelihoods of locals. Field Museum researchers found that local people in Calumet view "environment" more holistically than do many conservationists—integrating open space or natural area protection with health, safety, and other issues. In this sense, by paying attention to broader ecological issues, such as contamination issues and remediation (that benefit peoples' health as well as biodiversity), conservationists are more likely to get people to support the conservation issues—a "natural" alliance can be formed between local residents and conservationists.

Urban areas make the connection between social issues and conservation biology particularly clear. But even in pure conservation terms, the patches between smokestacks and abandoned factories, between loading docks and rivers, along freight lines and next to landfills, can provide rich opportunities to preserve and increase biodiversity. These are opportunities best not ignored.

LITERATURE CITED

Blus, L.J.; Henny, C.J.; Anderson, A.; Fitzner, R.E. 1985. Reproduction, mortality, and heavy metal concentrations in great blue herons from three colonies in Washington and Idaho. Colonial Waterbirds. 8: 110-116.

City of Chicago Department of Environment. 2002. Calumet Area Ecological Management Strategy. Chicago: City of Chicago, Department of Environment. 170 p. [Available online: http://www.ncrs.fs.fed.us/4902/focus/calumet/recovery/default.asp]

City of Chicago Department of Planning and Development. 2002. Calumet Land Use Plan. Chicago: City of Chicago. 16 p.

Custer, T.W.; Hensler, G.L.; Earl, T.E. 1983. Clutch size, reproductive success, and organochlorine contaminants in Atlantic coast black-crowned night-herons. Auk. 100: 699-710.

Custer, T.W.; Bickham, J.W.; Lyne, T.B.; et al. 1994. Flow cytometry for monitoring contaminant exposure in black-crowned night-herons. Archives of Environmental Contamination and Toxicology. 27: 176-179.

Custer, T.W.; Hines, R.K.; Melancon, M.J.; et al. 1997. Contaminant concentrations and biomarker response in great blue heron eggs from 10 colonies on the Upper Mississippi River, USA. Environmental Toxicology and Chemistry. 16: 260-271.

Deason, J.P.; Sherk, G.W.; Carroll, G.A. 2001. Public policies and private decisions affecting the redevelopment of brownfields: an analysis of critical factors, relative weights and areal differentials. Report submitted to: U.S. Environmental Protection Agency, Office of Solid Waste and Emergency Response. [Available online: http://www.gwu.edu/~eem/Brownfields/index.htm]

Findholt, S.L.; Trost, C.H. 1985. Organochlorine pollutants, eggshell thickness, and reproductive success of black-crowned night-herons in Idaho. Colonial Waterbirds. 8: 32-41.

Fleming, W.J.; Pullin, B.P.; Swineford, D.M. 1984. Population trends and environmental contaminants in herons in the Tennessee valley, 1980-81. Colonial Waterbirds. 7: 63-73.

Halbrook, R.S.; Brewer, R.L.; Buehler, D.A. 1999. Ecological risk assessments on a large river-reservoir: 7. Environmental contaminant accumulation and effects in Great Blue Heron. Environmental Toxicology and Chemistry. 18: 641-648.

Henny, C.J.; Blus, L.J.; Krynitsky, A.J.; Bunck, C.M. 1984. Current impact of DDE on black-crowned night-herons in the Intermountain West. Journal of Wildlife Management. 48: 1-13.

Hoffman, D.J.; Rattner, B.A.; Bunck, C.M.; et al. 1986. Association between PCBs and lower embryonic weight in black-crowned night-herons in San Francisco Bay. Journal of Toxicology and Environmental Health. 19: 383-391.

Hothem, R.L.; Roster, D.L.; King, K.A.; et al. 1995. Spatial and temporal trends of contaminants in eggs of wading birds from San Francisco Bay, California. Environmental Toxicology and Chemistry. 14: 1319-1331.

Jones, E.L. 1998. From steel town to "ghost town": a qualitative study of community change in southeast Chicago. Masters thesis. Chicago, IL: Loyola University, Department of Sociology. 108 p.

Kretzmann, J.P.; McKnight, J.L. 1993. Building communities from the inside out: a path toward finding and mobilizing a community's assets. Evanston, IL: Asset-Based Community Development Institute, Northwestern University. 376 p.

Northeast Midwest Institute. 2001. Brownfield basics: an issue primer. Washington, DC: Northeast Midwest Institute. 5 p. [Available online: http://www.nemw.org/BFprimer.pdf]

Ohlendorf, H.M.; Klaas, E.E.; Kaiser, T.E. 1978. Environmental pollutants and eggshell thinning in the black-crowned night heron. In: Sprint, A.; Ogden, J.C.D.; Winkler, S., eds. Wading birds. Research Report 7. New York, NY: National Audubon Society: 63-82.

Price, I.M. 1977. Environmental contaminants in relation to Canadian wildlife. Transactions of the North American Wildlife and Natural Resources Conference. 42: 382-396.

Proshansky, H.M. 1976. The appropriation and misappropriation of space. In: Korosec-Serfaty, P., ed. Appropriation of space. Proceedings of the Strasbourg Conference. Louvain-la-Neuve, Belgium: CIACO: 31-45

Rattner, B.A.; Melancon, M.J.; Rice, C.P.; et al. 1997. Cytochrome P450 and organochlorine contaminants in black-crowned night-herons from the Chesapeake Bay region, USA. Environmental Toxicology and Chemistry. 16: 2315-2322.

Rattner, B.A.; Hoffman, D.J.; Melancon, M.J.; et al. 2000. Organochlorine and metal contaminant exposure and effects in hatching black-crowned night-herons (Nycticorax nycticorax) in Delaware Bay. Archives of Environmental Contamination and Toxicology. 39: 38-45.

U.S. Department of the Interior, National Park Service Midwest Region. 1998. Calumet ecological park feasibility study. Omaha, NE: USDI, National Park Service Midwest Region. 73 p.

Seoul's Greenbelt: An Experiment in Urban Containment

David N. Bengston[1] and Youn Yeo-Chang[2]

ABSTRACT—Urban containment policies are considered by some to be a promising approach to growth management. The greenbelt-based urban containment policy of Seoul, Republic of Korea is examined as a case study. Seoul's greenbelt has generated both significant social costs and benefits. Korea's greenbelt policy is currently being revised, largely due to pressure from greenbelt landowners and developers. While there is no definitive answer to the question of whether Seoul would be a more or less "sustainable city" today without the greenbelt, it is certain that in the absence of the greenbelt Seoul would have lost much of its rich natural heritage and essential ecosystem services.

Countries around the world have responded to growing concern about the problems associated with sprawling development patterns by creating a wide range of policy instruments designed to manage urban growth and protect open space (Bengston et al. 2004, Richardson and Bae 2004). But the effectiveness of these policies is often questioned. Innovative and effective policies will be required to stem the tide of increasingly land-consumptive development. Out of the array of growth management techniques, urban containment policies are considered by some to be a promising approach. National urban containment policies have been in place for many decades in a few countries, including the United Kingdom and the Republic of Korea. In the United States, local urban containment programs have typically been created by individual municipalities without direction or assistance from state or national governments (Dawkins and Nelson 2002).

Pendall et al. (2002) distinguished three types of urban containment policies: greenbelts, urban growth boundaries, and urban service boundaries. A greenbelt refers to a physical area of open space–farmland, forest, or other greenspace–that surrounds a city or metropolitan area and is intended to be a permanent barrier to urban expansion. Development is strictly regulated or prohibited on greenbelt land. Greenbelts may be created through public or nonprofit acquisition of open space or development rights, as in Boulder, Colorado (Pollock 1998), or they may be created and enforced by regulation of private property. Voters in Ann Arbor, Michigan, recently overwhelmingly approved a greenbelt proposal that will involve purchase of both land and development rights (Ann Arbor News 2003). Greenbelts have rarely been used in the United States but have been used much more extensively in large cities in Europe and Asia. London was the first major city to introduce a greenbelt system in the late 1930s (Munton 1983). Other cities that have adopted (or adopted and subsequently abandoned)

greenbelts include Ottawa and three other Canadian cities (Taylor et al. 1995); Asian megacities including Tokyo, Seoul, and Bangkok (Yokohari et al. 2000); and many large European cities such as Berlin, Vienna, Barcelona, and Budapest (Kuhn 2003).

In contrast to greenbelts, an urban growth boundary (UGB) is not a physical space but a dividing line drawn around an urban area to separate it from surrounding rural areas. Zoning and other regulatory tools are used to implement a UGB. Areas outside the boundary are zoned for rural uses and the area inside is zoned for urban use. A key distinction between UGBs and greenbelts is that the former are not intended to be permanent. A UGB is typically drawn to accommodate expected growth for some period of time, and the boundary is reassessed and expanded as needed. In Oregon, the Land Conservation and Development Act of 1973 required, among other things, the delineation of urban growth boundaries around all of the state's cities and around the Portland metropolitan area (Nelson 1994).

Urban service boundaries, the third type of urban containment policy, are even more flexible than UGBs. An urban service boundary delineates the area beyond which certain urban services such as sewer and water will not be provided. They are often linked with adequate public facilities ordinances that prohibit development in areas not served by specific public services and facilities. Assessments of urban service boundaries have generally found them to be of limited effectiveness in containing sprawl, in part because they tend to be easily and frequently amended in the face of political pressure to accommodate growth (e.g., Dearborn and Gygi 1993, Poradek 1997).

This paper focuses on greenbelts, the most restrictive form of urban containment policy. The idea of surrounding cities with a belt of agricultural land or other open space is an ancient one, dating back at least to the 13th century B.C.

[1] USDA Forest Service, North Central Research Station, 1992 Folwell Avenue, St. Paul, MN 55108; e-mail: dbengston@fs.fed.us

[2] Department of Forest Science, Seoul National University, San 56-1 Shillim-dong, Gwanak-gu, Seoul, 151-742 Republic of Korea; e-mail: youn@snu.ac.kr

Citation for proceedings: Bengston, David N., tech. ed. 2005. Policies for managing urban growth and landscape change: a key to conservation in the 21st Century. Gen. Tech. Rep. NC-265. St. Paul, MN: U.S. Department of Agriculture, Forest Service, North Central Research Station. 51 p.

and the Levitical cities of Palestine (Ginsberg 1956, Osborn 1969). In more recent times, greenbelts were proposed in the influential work of Sir Ebenezer Howard in 1898 (Howard 1902), and they have been a widely used policy in some countries for containing urban expansion, protecting agricultural land and open spaces, and achieving other public goals. Greenbelts have long been a controversial public policy because of their purported negative consequences, including increased land and housing prices in the urban area contained by the greenbelt, decreased greenbelt land prices, loss or restriction of development rights for greenbelt landowners, increased urban congestion, and other undesirable consequences. Greenbelts also have been accused of causing sprawl and higher commuting costs as development jumps over the greenbelt. But greenbelts also generate significant social and environmental benefits, including amenity and recreational value, bequest value, and protection of open space, agricultural land, natural resources, and life-supporting ecosystem services.

We examine the longstanding greenbelt surrounding Seoul, Republic of Korea. Some have suggested that, overall, Seoul's greenbelt is a rare success in urban containment: "The greenbelt in Seoul, so far, may be evaluated as one of few successful greenbelt experiences in Asia," (Yokohari *et al.* 2000: 163). Others claim the social costs of Seoul's greenbelt have overwhelmed the benefits and the policy should be abandoned. The debate about Seoul's greenbelt policy is part of a broader debate among urban planners about the desirability and sustainability of compact cities (e.g., Gordon and Richardson 1997, Jenks *et al.* 1996).

The following sections describe the context and history of Seoul's greenbelt, briefly summarize its costs and benefits, and discuss recent major reforms in the policy. A concluding section discusses lessons from the Korean experience and relevance for growth management in other countries.

SEOUL'S GREENBELT POLICY

Korea's greenbelt system was introduced in 1971 during the authoritarian government of President Park Chung Hee. The social context for this policy was extremely rapid economic and population growth (Song 2003) and a high rate of rural-urban migration. Seoul grew more rapidly than any city in the world from 1950 to 1975, growing at an average annual rate of 7.6 percent (UN Population Division 2002). Seoul's population grew from just over a million in 1950 to more than 6.8 million in 1975. By 2000, the population of Seoul was about 10 million, but the population of the entire Capital Region (Gyeonggi Province, including the city of Inchon) had ballooned to more than 21 million.

Seoul's greenbelt was patterned after the greenbelt of London (Bae 1998) but adapted in the Korean context. Greenbelts, formally referred to as Restricted Development Zones (RDZs) in Korea, were introduced in the City Planning Law of 1971 and shaped by the 1972-1981 National Comprehensive Physical Plan of 1973 (Lee 2000, 2004). Greenbelts were designated around Seoul and 13 other cities between 1971 and 1973.

Seoul's greenbelt is very large, consisting of a band averaging about 10 km wide that begins about 15 km from Seoul's central business district (fig. 1). After being extended four times by 1976, Seoul's greenbelt contained 1,566.8 square km, about 13.3 percent of the Seoul Metropolitan Area. The population living within the greenbelt is small, however, accounting for only 1.66 percent of the Seoul Metropolitan Area's population (Bae and Jun 2003). Most development has been strictly prohibited on greenbelt land and greenbelt landowners have received no compensation for their loss of development rights (Bae 1998, Lee 1999). The economic hardship imposed on landowners has been contentious from the beginning, because nationwide about 80 percent of the land within greenbelts is privately owned (Lee 2000, 2004). The boundaries of Korea's greenbelts were hastily drawn without public input and without serious consideration of widely accepted criteria for the designation of greenbelts. In one case, a village was divided down the middle by the greenbelt boundary (Choe 2004b).

Bae (1998) identified seven objectives for the establishment of Seoul's greenbelt. First, unlike greenbelts in most countries, national security was originally a dominant objective. Given the perceived threat of invasion from North Korea, the greenbelt allowed the government to strictly control development near the Demilitarized Zone north of Seoul. Choe (2004a) noted that more than 40 percent of South Korea's population was living within range of a ground artillery attack from North Korea in the early 1970s. Second, greenbelt regulations were used as a means to eradicate illegal shantytowns on the outskirts of Seoul. Third, the greenbelt was viewed as a way to control urban sprawl. Government efforts to control the rapid expansion of Seoul during the 1960s had been ineffective (Kim and Kim 2000). A fourth objective was to reduce rapid growth in population and industrial concentration in the Capital Region. Fifth, expansion of the greenbelt was viewed as a way to limit land speculation in the metropolitan region. Sixth, the greenbelt was intended to protect agricultural land and promote food security. Finally, environmental and natural resource protection also was an objective of the greenbelt policy.

The relative importance of these objectives has changed over time. For example, the importance of environmental protection as a rationale for the greenbelt has grown significantly as environmental awareness and economic prosperity in Korea have increased (Lee 2000, 2004). An additional and increasingly important rationale for Seoul's greenbelt is the provision of recreational resources to a city short of parks and nongreenbelt open space. Almost three-fifths of Seoul's greenbelt consists of mountains and forests that are heavily used for recreation (Bae and Jun 2003).

Korea's greenbelt policy has enjoyed great support from the general public (Kim and Kim 2000). Lee (1999) cited several surveys conducted in the 1990s that found strong support from citizens, environmentalists, and Korean planners, but opposition from most greenbelt property owners who viewed the policy as seizure of private property. A 1998 survey conducted by the Ministry of Construction and Transportation (MOCT) found that most government officials and academics preferred to retain the greenbelt, but they felt reforms were

Figure 1.—The Capital Region (Gyeonggi Province) and Seoul's greenbelt.

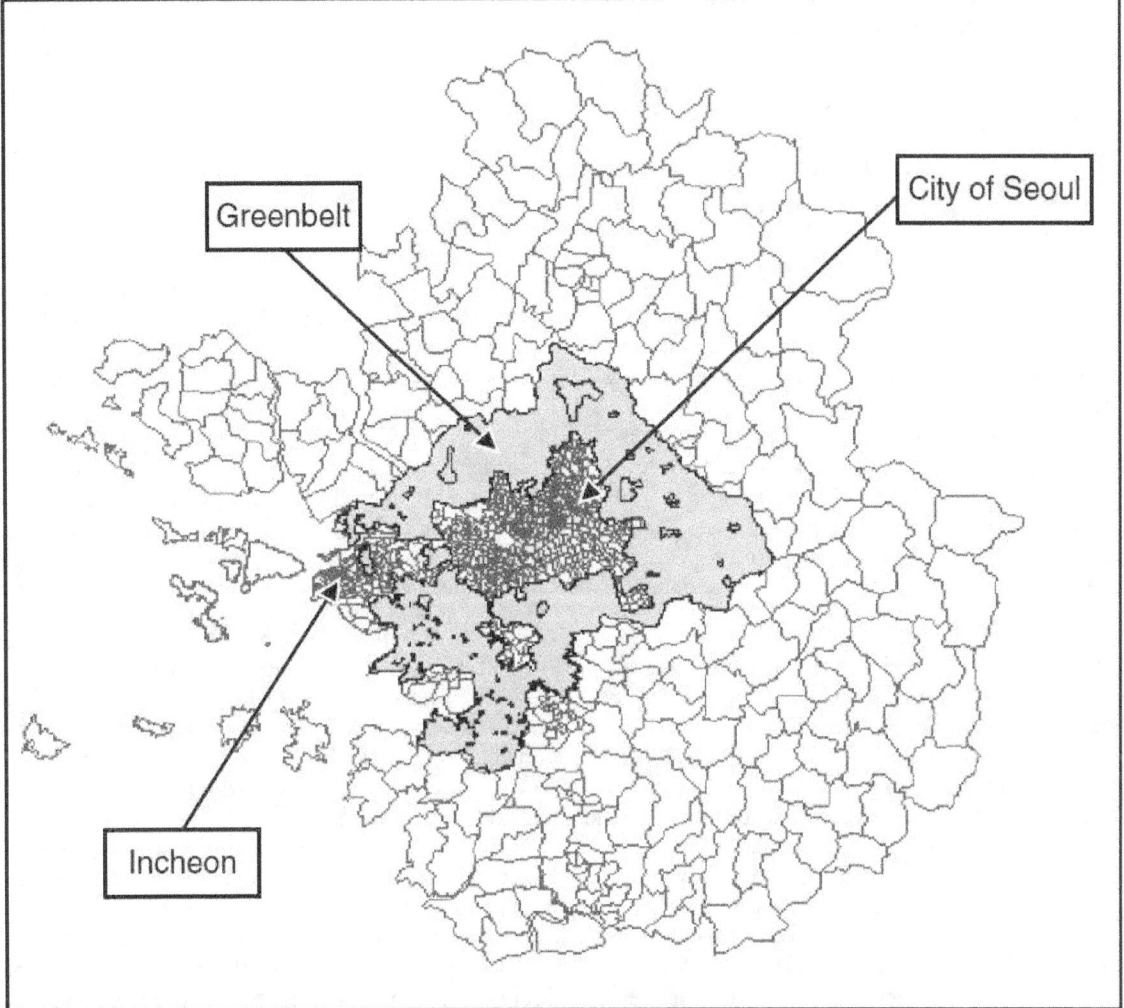

needed to ensure the achievement of development goals (MOCT 1998). Lee (2004) carried out a multivariate analysis of the data from the 1998 MOCT national survey to account for variation in greenbelt support. He found greater support for the greenbelt policy by individuals with higher incomes and educational attainment, and lower support by individuals residing in regions with strong development pressure and in the Capital Region. Surprisingly, he did not find a statistically significant relationship between opposition to the policy and ownership of land within greenbelt boundaries.

COSTS AND BENEFITS OF SEOUL'S GREENBELT

Cheshire and Sheppard (2002) noted that most economic research on land use planning has focused on the costs and neglected the benefits. This is true for economic research on Seoul's greenbelt policy. Most of the economic studies of Seoul's greenbelt have focused on its social costs, especially higher land prices, housing prices, and commuting costs. Several studies have examined the decrease in the price of nongreenbelt land and housing that would result from either a partial relaxation or complete elimination of the greenbelt (e.g., Choi 1994, Kim 1993, Kim et al. 1986). These studies found relatively modest

effects of the greenbelt on land and housing prices. For example, Choi (1994) estimated that land prices in the greenbelt in 1987 were about 30 percent below non-greenbelt land values, a much smaller price differential than suggested by anecdotal reports. Choi's analysis also indicated that if Seoul's greenbelt had been completely eliminated in 1987, greenbelt land prices would have risen by an average of 32.1 percent and nongreenbelt prices would have fallen by 7.5 percent.

It is important to recognize that Seoul's greenbelt policy is but one of many supply-side restrictions that put upward pressure on land and housing prices. A variety of other government policies may restrict land and housing supply, including multiple layers of urban zoning, agricultural zoning, a virtual public monopoly on urban land development, the system of land and housing taxation, and an inadequate system of housing finance (Choi 1993; Kim 1990, 1993). Hannah et al. (1993) concluded that the government's tendency to underallocate land to urban residential use was responsible for a substantial part of the increase in urban housing prices. Demand-side factors, such as the local and regional amenities provided by greenbelts, also put upward pressure on land and housing prices by shifting the demand curves for land and housing outward.

Several studies have examined the additional costs incurred by commuters who live beyond the greenbelt and work in Seoul. For example, Han (1997) estimated the social costs associated with Seoul's greenbelt and found increased travel costs were the largest component. Additional travel costs–excluding the value of commuters' time–were estimated at $192 (250,000 won) per person per year, or $3.6 billion (470 billion won) total per year. A lower estimate of the additional travel costs, including the value of commuters' time, was about 365 billion won per year in the late 1980s (Kim 1993). See Jun and Bae (2000) and Jun and Hur (2001) for additional estimates of commuting costs associated with Seoul's greenbelt.

Greenbelts may provide three broad categories of benefits: (1) amenity value related to scenic beauty, recreational opportunities, and bequest/heritage value; (2) fiscal savings due to increased efficiency in the provision of public services and infrastructure associated with more compact development; and perhaps most significantly (3) a wide range of ecosystem services such as air purification, habitat and biodiversity protection, flood control, and water supply and quality. The few studies of the benefits of Seoul's greenbelt have looked only at part of the first benefit category and neglected the other two categories.

Strong evidence has been found that greenbelts generate an amenity value to nearby urban land (e.g., Correll et al. 1978; Knaap and Nelson 1988; Nelson 1986, 1988), and a large body of literature documents the significant impact of open space on residential property values (see Fausold and Lilieholm 1996, and studies cited therein). A few studies have explored the amenity benefits of Seoul's greenbelt. An econometric analysis by Lee and Linneman (1998) found significant amenity value, although the benefits began to decrease after 1980 due to congestion effects. Lee and Fujita (1997) demonstrated theoretically that, depending on the nature of the greenbelt amenity, there are circumstances in which residential development jumping over a greenbelt could be economically efficient (i.e., the social benefits of the greenbelt outweigh its social costs). This is due to the amenity value to residents living both inside and outside the greenbelt.

The bequest and heritage values of Seoul's greenbelt and the desire of many citizens to pass on this natural heritage to future generations are likely to be significant (Jin and Park 2000), but they have not been studied. Seoul's greenbelt has an ancient historical precedent: the first king of the Choson Dynasty (1392-1910) prohibited all types of land utilization and development on the mountains around Seoul by royal proclamation in 1397 (Han 1992). In addition, village groves have an ancient history in traditional Korean village life (Park and Lee 2002). For many centuries these groves had great spiritual, social, and ecological significance. Village groves served as small greenbelts, separating villages from agricultural fields and preventing the encroachment of villages into farmland. Thus, the current greenbelt system is linked to Korea's history and deeply held cultural values.

No studies have estimated the fiscal savings attributable to Seoul's greenbelt due to increased efficiency in the provision of public infrastructure (such as roads, water and sewer systems, and schools) although this may be a significant source of benefits.

There is general but not universal agreement in the empirical literature on the costs of urban sprawl that development density is linked to infrastructure costs, with lower costs associated with higher density (Burchell et al. 1998, 2002). Seoul is among the most densely populated cities in the world in part due to its greenbelt, and hence the fiscal savings may be substantial.

Finally, although the ecosystem service benefits of Seoul's greenbelt have not been analyzed, an abundance of other literature suggests the importance–and perhaps the primacy–of this category of benefits. Yokohari et al. (1994) identified 26 ecological functions of farmland and forests that provide benefits to urban areas, all of which are relevant for greenbelts. Greenbelts of various types have been recognized for their flood control benefits (Yokohari et al. 2000), their effect on controlling summer heat in surrounding residential areas (Yokohari et al. 1997; see also Koh et al. 1999), air pollution abatement (Khan and Abbasi 2000a, 2000b), and their use as habitat for endangered species (Mortberg and Wallentinus 2000). The well-known case of the New York City watershed (Daily and Ellison 2002) suggests the substantial economic value of watershed services (water quality and quantity) that may be provided by greenbelts.

In a rare study that examined whether Seoul's greenbelt provides a net benefit, Lee (1999) estimated the net social gain arising from a marginal release of greenbelt land for development. Lee calculated net benefits at four points in time: 1975, 1980, 1984, and 1989. Although this analysis required many simplifying assumptions and did not include important benefit categories, it did shed light on how the economic effects of a greenbelt change as the metropolitan area grows and the impacts of an increasingly restricted land supply and growing congestion are felt. Lee found that Seoul's greenbelt policy was inefficient in 1975 (i.e., the benefits of a marginal release of greenbelt land outweighed the costs), was efficient in 1980 and 1984 as amenity benefits increased significantly, and became inefficient again in 1989 as continuing urban growth created congestion costs that overwhelmed the amenity benefits. He concluded that a fixed greenbelt cannot provide net benefits indefinitely in the context of rapid urban growth, i.e., "… a greenbelt is just a congestible local public good," (p. 49). Lee did not consider benefits associated with greenbelt recreation, greater efficiency in providing public infrastructure, or ecosystem services, however, which are all likely to *increase* with continued urban growth.

GREENBELT POLICY REFORM

From its beginning in 1971, Seoul's greenbelt policy remained essentially unchanged for almost 30 years. Public discussion of problems associated with the greenbelt was prohibited during the Park regime (Lee and Linneman 1998), which lasted until 1979. Subsequent military governments continued the greenbelt policy. Hence, opposition to the greenbelt was rarely expressed in the early years. But opposition from greenbelt landowners began to be voiced after the current civilian republic was established in 1988 (Park 2001). During the presidential election of 1997, opposition party candidate Kim Dae Jung made a campaign promise to review and reform the greenbelt policy (Choe 2004a). After winning the election,

Kim Dae Jung established a National Committee for Green Belt Policy Reform early in 1998. The committee, chaired by Prof. Choe Sang-Chuel of Seoul National University, consisted of three greenbelt residents, one environmental group representative, twelve scholars, three government officials, and three journalists (Park 2001).

After a difficult, yearlong process of meetings and deliberations, the committee submitted a draft report to the MOCT on November 24, 1998. The report recommended the following reforms (Choe 2004a): (1) The greenbelt policy should be maintained as a growth management tool, but greenbelts should be lifted around small and medium cities with little development pressure and replaced with conventional zoning regulations; (2) in large cities that retain greenbelts, the boundaries should be re-delineated based on environmental assessments and consideration of other local factors; (3) a scheme for the government to recoup windfall benefits due to abolishing or relaxing greenbelts should be introduced to prevent land speculation; (4) landowners in areas that remain greenbelts should be compensated for their loss of development rights or offered the option of having their land purchased by the government at a fair price; (5) villages above a certain size within greenbelts should be given special permission for developments needed to improve their communities.

Release of the draft report generated conflict. On the day the report was issued, a group called National Action for Greenbelt (NAG) was established (Park 2001). NAG supported preservation of the greenbelt and used diverse tactics in an attempt to derail reform. For example, NAG investigated members of the MOCT committee of the National Assembly to find out if any of them owned greenbelt land, and they found that 6 out of 30 members were indeed landowners. They also used the press effectively to gain public support for preserving the greenbelts.

The MOCT held a series of public hearings to discuss the draft report in greenbelt cities across Korea in late November and early December of 1998. Greenbelt residents who were unhappy that the report did not recommend complete removal of Seoul's greenbelt disrupted the public hearing held in Seoul. In response to the growing conflict, the MOCT requested a commentary on the draft report from the British Town and Country Planning Association (TCPA) on December 12, 1998.[3] The TCPA commentary was released on June 3, 1999, and generated divergent views about whether or not it supported the reforms recommended by the National Committee for Green Belt Policy Reform (Park 2001).

While conflict among greenbelt stakeholders raged, a committee consisting of delegates from the MOCT, the Korea Research Institute for Human Settlements, and other research institutes was established to work out practical and legal details of greenbelt reform (Choe 2004a). But because they were unable to reach agreement among stakeholders, the MOCT unilaterally announced the new RDZ policy on July 22, 1999. The committee recommended eliminating greenbelts around seven small and medium cities and rezoning the

land as either conservation-green areas or natural-green areas, zoning categories from Korea's City Planning Law. Greenbelts in the seven larger cities would be maintained but redrawn based on environmental assessment that included factors such as topography, land suitability, ecological sensitivity, and environmental vulnerability (Choe 2004a). In these seven cities, the greenbelt boundaries are to be redrawn using metropolitan area-wide planning. Trying to reach agreement between the many municipal governments in the Capital Region has proven to be difficult. An effort to develop a metropolitan area plan for the Capital Region began in 2002 and may not be completed until 2005 or 2006 (S.C. Choe 2004, personal communication). In the meantime, a total of 112.5 square km of Seoul's greenbelt has been proposed for release. This land would be made available for development according to the 15-year metropolitan plan rather than all at once (Bae and Jun 2003).

Opposition to the release of land from Seoul's greenbelt from environmental groups and many residents of Seoul has continued in recent years as proposals for development have moved forward. This is reflected in news media discussion of greenbelt reform. For example, an editorial discussing a plan by the Seoul Metropolitan Government to construct 100,000 apartment units on land currently in the greenbelt mentioned the protests that have taken place and stated

… city hall and the central government should have first considered the unavoidable damage that will be done to the greenbelt, which acts as the lungs of the city. Needless to say, if the greenbelt turns into a forest of apartments under the development project, the overpopulation of the capital city will certainly worsen, while residents will also lose the small amount of natural environment that still exists (Korea Times 2003).

An editorial in another newspaper stated that "… Seoul's green belt has been protected so far because there are more merits than demerits in maintaining it. We have to continue to be careful about damaging it. Destruction of nature for housing development and subsequent traffic congestion is not a net gain in our welfare" (JoongAng Daily 2003).

CONCLUSIONS

Bruegmann (2001) characterized the effectiveness and effects of London's greenbelt system–the main inspiration for Seoul's greenbelt–as follows: "This system… did in fact stop much, although not all, of the growth that otherwise might have invaded the greenbelt around London. It was not nearly as successful in containing growth beyond the belt. In fact, growth beyond the greenbelt eventually scattered across much of southeast England" (p.16,090).

This statement could have been written about Seoul's greenbelt except that Seoul's strictly enforced policy has been much more effective at keeping development (other than agricultural use) out of the greenbelt. But Seoul's urban containment policy largely failed to keep development from invading the Capital Region beyond the greenbelt. The intense pressure of exceptionally rapid urban growth was simply too much to

---

[3] Founded in 1899 to promote Ebenezer Howard's Garden City concept, the TCPA is Britain's oldest non-governmental organization concerned with planning and the environment.

contain. The result has been a physical footprint (the area of land taken up by the entire metropolitan region) that is probably larger than would have been the case in the absence of the greenbelt (Bae and Jun 2003). But Seoul's greenbelt has been remarkably successful at protecting important agricultural land, providing badly needed recreational resources in a megacity with few parks, protecting the beauty and natural heritage of the ancient capital of Korea, and maintaining vital ecosystem services.

A lesson of this review is that urban containment policies lead to both significant benefits and costs, and that these costs and benefits change over time with population and economic growth. A number of researchers have concluded that the social costs of Seoul's policy could have been reduced if the greenbelt had been more flexible and had accommodated growth, similar to most urban growth boundaries in the U.S. For example, in discussing the implications of Seoul's policy, Dawkins and Nelson (2002: 6-7) stated that "… urban containment boundaries should be periodically re-evaluated and extended to allow for sufficient land release. If the boundary is not periodically revised, net social benefits will be offset by the increased social costs associated with congestion externalities and land supply constraints" (see also Jun and Hur 2001: 158, Lee 1999: 50). This view represents the conventional wisdom of the urban planning profession: growth accommodation is always the preferred policy (Zovanyi, this volume).

But this view fails to account for what are likely the most significant categories of benefits associated with Seoul's greenbelt: the life supporting ecosystem services and recreational resources it provides to residents of the Seoul Metropolitan Area. The value of these benefits will likely rise with continued growth and urbanization. Therefore, whether or not Seoul's greenbelt has provided net benefits to society remains an open question. Few studies have empirically examined the benefits of Seoul's greenbelt policy, and no studies have attempted to measure the economic value of its ecosystem services, recreational value, or bequest and heritage values.

Would Seoul be a more or less "sustainable city" today without the greenbelt? There is no definitive answer to this question. Despite the importance of moving toward more sustainable cities in our increasingly urbanized world, there is no consensus about the nature or dimensions of urban sustainability (Burton et al. 1996). Assessing urban sustainability is an extraordinarily complex task because of the complexity of cities: they consist of many layers of constantly changing economic, social, legal, cultural, political, and ecological systems. But we do know with certainty that in the absence of the greenbelt, Seoul would have lost much of its rich natural heritage and essential ecosystem services.

ACKNOWLEDGMENT

The authors thank the Organisation for Economic Co-operation and Development (OECD) Co-operative Research Programme, Biological Resource Management for Sustainable Agricultural Systems, for a fellowship that enabled Dr. Bengston to participate in this research effort. We also thank Professors Kai Lee and Casey Dawkins for helpful comments on an earlier version of this paper.

LITERATURE CITED

Ann Arbor News. 2003. Greenbelt proposal wins landslide voter approval. Ann Arbor News, November 5. [Available online: http://www.mlive.com/aanews/]

Bae, C.H.C. 1998. Korea's greenbelts: impacts and options for change. Pacific Rim Law & Policy Journal. 7(3): 479-502.

Bae, C.H.C.; Jun, M.J. 2003. Counterfactual planning: What if there had been no greenbelt in Seoul? Journal of Planning Education and Research. 22(4): 374-383.

Bengston, D.N.; Fletcher, J.; Nelson, K. 2004. Public policies for managing urban growth and protecting open space: policy instruments and lessons learned in the United States. Landscape and Urban Planning. 69: 271-286.

Bruegmann, R. 2001. Urban sprawl. International Encyclopedia of the Social & Behavioral Sciences. Online Edition, Elsevier Science, Ltd.: 16087-16082. [Available online: http://www.sciencedirect.com/science/reference-works/0080430767]

Burchell, R.W.; Lowenstein, G.; Dolphin, W.R., et al. 2002. Costs of sprawl – 2000. Report 74. Transit Cooperative Research Program, Transportation Research Board, National Research Council. Washington, DC: National Academy Press. 605 p. [Available online: http://www4.trb.org/trb/crp.nsf/All+Projects/TCRP+H-10]

Burchell, R.W.; Shad, N.A.; Listokin, D., et al. 1998. The costs of sprawl—revisited. Report 39. Transit Cooperative Research Program, Transportation Research Board, National Research Council. Washington, DC: National Academy Press. 268 p. [Available online: http://www4.trb.org/trb/crp.nsf/All+Projects/TCRP+H-10]

Burton, E.; Williams, K.; Jenks, M. 1996. The compact city and urban sustainability: conflicts and complexities. In: Jenks, M.; Burton, E.; Williams, K., eds. The compact city: a sustainable urban form? London, England: Chapman and Hall: 231-247.

Cheshire, P.; Sheppard, S. 2002. The welfare economics of land use planning. Journal of Urban Economics. 52: 242-269.

Choe, S.C. 2004a. Reform of planning controls for an urban-rural continuum in Korea. In: Sorensen, A.; Marcotullio, P.J.; Grant, J., eds. Towards sustainable cities: East Asian, North American and European perspectives on managing urban regions. Burlington, VT: Ashgate: 253-266.

Choe, S.C. 2004b. The thirty-year's experiment with British greenbelt policy in Korea: a convergent path to sustainable development. In: Richardson, H.W.; Bae, C.H.C., eds. Urban sprawl in Western Europe and the United States. Burlington, VT: Ashgate: 83-90.

Choi, M.J. 1993. Spatial and temporal variations in land values: a descriptive and behavioral analysis of the Seoul Metropolitan Area (1956-1989). Cambridge, MA: Harvard University. 178 p. Ph.D. dissertation.

Choi, M.J. 1994. An empirical analysis of the impacts of green-belt on land prices in the Seoul Metropolitan Area. Korean Journal of Urban Planning. 29(2): 97-111. In Korean.

Correll, M.R.; Lillydahl, J.H.; Singell, L.D. 1978. The effects of greenbelts on residential property values: some findings on the political economy of open space. Land Economics. 54: 207-217.

Daily, G.C.; Ellison, K. 2002. The new economy of nature: the quest to make conservation profitable. Washington, DC: Island Press/Shearwater Books. 260 p.

Dawkins, C.J.; Nelson, A.C. 2002. Urban containment policies and housing prices: an international comparison with implications for future research. Land Use Policy. 19: 1-12.

Dearborn, K.W.; Gygi, A.M. 1993. Planner's panacea or Pandora's box: a realistic assessment of the role of urban growth areas in achieving growth management goals. Puget Sound Law Review. 16: 975-1023.

Fausold, C.J.; Lilieholm, R.J. 1996. The economic value of open space: a review and synthesis. Working Paper WP96CF1. Cambridge, MA: Lincoln Institute of Land Policy. 40 p.

Ginsburg, L. 1956. Green belts in the Bible. Journal of the Town Planning Institute. 42(May): 129-130.

Gordon, P.; Richardson, H.W. 1997. Are compact cities a desirable planning goal? Journal of the American Planning Association. 63(1): 95-106.

Han, D.W. 1992. The location and functions of Keumsan in Seoul of the early Choson Dynasty. Seoul: Seoul National University. In Korean with English abstract. 77 p. Master's thesis.

Han, S. 1997. Measuring the social cost of green belt zoning. Research Report 1997-03-19. Seoul: Korea Economic Research Institute. 39 p.

Hannah, L.; Kim, K.H.; Mills, E.S. 1993. Land use controls and housing prices in Korea. Urban Studies. 30(1): 147-156.

Howard, E. 1902. Garden cities of to-morrow. London, England: Sonnenschein & Co. (First published in 1898 as: To-morrow: a peaceful path to real reform). 125 p.

Jenks, M.; Burton, E.; Williams, K., eds. 1996. The compact city: a sustainable urban form? London, England: Chapman and Hall. 350 p.

Jin, Y.H.; Park, J.G. 2000. The reform of green belt policy: Korean experiences. In: Papers and Proceedings of the International Workshop on Urban Growth Management Policies of Korea, Japan and U.S.A. June 23-24, 2000. Seoul, Korea: Korean Regional Science Association and Korea Research Institute for Human Settlements: 125-139.

JoongAng Daily. 2003. Green belt erosion (editorial). December 29, 2003. [Available online: http://joongangdaily.joins.com/]

Jun, M.J.; C. Bae. 2000. Estimating the commuting costs of Seoul's greenbelt. International Regional Science Review. 23(3): 300-315.

Jun, M.J.; Hur, J.W. 2001. Commuting costs of "leap-frog" newtown development in Seoul. Cities. 18(3): 151-158.

Khan, F.I.; Abbasi, S.A. 2000a. Attenuation of gaseous pollutants by greenbelts. Environmental Monitoring and Assessment. 64: 457-475.

Khan, F.I.; Abbasi, S.A. 2000b. Cushioning the impact of toxic release from runaway industrial accidents with greenbelts. Journal of Loss Prevention in the Process Industries. 13(2): 109-124.

Kim, C.H.; Kim, K.H. 2000. The political economy of Korean government policies on real estate. Urban Studies. 37(7): 1157-1169.

Kim, K.H. 1990. An analysis of inefficiency due to inadequate mortgage financing: the case of Seoul, Korea. Journal of Urban Economics. 28(3): 371-390.

Kim, K.H. 1993. Housing prices, affordability, and government policy in Korea. Journal of Real Estate Finance and Economics. 6: 55-71.

Kim, K.H.; Mills, E.; Song, B.N. 1986. Korean government policies toward Seoul's greenbelt. Working Paper 86-2. Seoul: Korea Research Institute for Human Settlements. 29 p.

Knaap, G.J.; Nelson, A.C. 1988. The effects of regional land use control in Oregon: a theoretical and empirical review. The Review of Regional Studies. 18: 37-46.

Koh, K.S.; Kim, M.H.; Kim, J.H., et al. 1999. Evaluation on the environment amelioration functions of green spaces in Chongju city by GIS. Korean Society of Environmental Impact Assessment. 8(1): 51-59. In Korean with English abstract.

Korea Times. 2003. Seoul City's short-sightedness: don't turn greenbelt into apartment complex (editorial). December 26. [Available online: http://times.hankooki.com/]

Kuhn, M. 2003. Greenbelt and green heart: separating and integrating landscapes in European city regions. Landscape and Urban Planning. 64: 19-27.

Lee, C.M. 1999. An intertemporal efficiency test of a greenbelt: assessing the economic impacts of Seoul's greenbelt. Journal of Planning Education and Research. 19(1): 41-52.

Lee, C.M.; Fujita, M. 1997. Efficient configuration of a green-belt: Theoretical modeling of greenbelt amenity. Environment and Planning A. 29(11): 1999-2017.

Lee, C.M.; Linneman, P. 1998. Dynamics of the greenbelt amenity effect on the land market: the case of Seoul's green-belt. Real Estate Economics. 26(1): 107-129.

Lee, S.C. 2000. Measuring acceptance of regulatory growth management policy: Korea's green belt case. Seattle, WA: University of Washington. 251 p. Ph.D. dissertation.

Lee, S.C. 2004. Measuring public support for the Korean green belt policy: a multivariate analysis. Unpublished paper presented at the Association of Collegiate Schools of Planning 45th Annual Conference, Portland, OR, October 21-24, 2004.

Ministry of Construction and Transportation (MOCT). 1998. A survey for reform of the Restricted Development Zone. Seoul: MOCT. In Korean.

Mortberg, U.; Wallentinus, H.G. 2000. Red-listed forest bird species in an urban environment–assessment of green space corridors. Landscape and Urban Planning. 50(4): 215-226.

Munton, R. 1983. London's green belt: containment in practice. London, England: George Allen & Unwin. 178 p.

Nelson, A.C. 1986. Using land markets to evaluate urban containment programs. Journal of the American Planning Association. 52: 156-170.

Nelson, A.C. 1988. An empirical note on how regional urban containment policy influences an interaction between greenbelt and exurban land markets. Journal of the American Planning Association. 54: 178-184.

Nelson, A.C. 1994. Oregon's urban growth boundary policy as a landmark planning tool. In: Abbott, C.; Howe, D.; Adler, S., eds. Planning the Oregon way: a twenty-year evaluation. Corvallis, OR: Oregon State University Press: 25-47.

Osborn, F.J. 1969. The green-belt principle: a note on its historical origins. In: Green-belt cities (new edition). New York: Schocken Books: Appendix I: 167-180. (Originally published in 1946).

Park, H. 2001. Environmentally friendly land use planning, property rights, and public participation in South Korea: a case study of greenbelt policy reform. Major paper for Master of Urban and Regional Planning. Blacksburg, VA: Virginia Polytechnic Institute and State University. 87 p. [Available online: http://scholar.lib.vt.edu/theses/available/etd-05232001-172303/]

Park, J.C.; Lee, S.H. 2002. Village forests of Chinan. Chinan Cultural Unit, Republic of Korea. In Korean. 127 p.

Pendall, R.; Martin, J.; Fulton, W. 2002. Holding the line: urban containment in the United States. Discussion Paper. Center on Urban and Metropolitan Policy. Washington, DC: The Brookings Institution. 45 p. [Available online: http://www.brook.edu/dybdocroot/ es/urban/publications/pendallfultoncontainment.pdf]

Pollock, P. 1998. Controlling sprawl in Boulder: benefits and pitfalls. Land Lines (Newsletter of the Lincoln Institute of Land Policy). 10(1): 1-3.

Poradek, J. 1997. Putting the use back in metropolitan land-use planning: private enforcement of urban sprawl control laws. Minnesota Law Review. 81: 1343-1375.

Richardson, H.W.; Bae, C.H.C., eds. 2004. Urban sprawl in Western Europe and the United States. Burlington, VT: Ashgate. 325 p.

Song, B.N. 2003. The rise of the Korean economy. 3rd ed. New York: Oxford University Press. 400 p.

Taylor, J.; Paine, C.; FitzGibbon, J. 1995. From greenbelt to greenways: four Canadian case studies. Landscape and Urban Planning. 33: 47-64.

UN Population Division, Department of Economic and Social Affairs. 2002. World urbanization prospects: the 2001 revision. United Nations Publication Sales No. E.02.XIII.16. New York: United Nations. [Available online: http://www.un.org/esa/population/publications/wup2001/WUP2001report.htm]

Yokohari, M.; Brown, R.D.; Takeuchi, K. 1994. A framework for the conservation of rural ecological landscapes in the urban fringe area in Japan. Landscape and Urban Planning. 29(2-3): 103-116.

Yokohari, M.; Brown, R.D.; Kato, Y.; Moriyama, H. 1997. Effects of paddy fields on summertime air and surface temperatures in urban fringe areas of Tokyo, Japan. Landscape and Urban Planning. 38(1-2): 1-11.

Yokohari, M.; Takeuchi, K.; Watanabe, T.; Yokota, S. 2000. Beyond greenbelts and zoning: a new planning concept for the environment of Asian mega-cities. Landscape and Urban Planning. 47: 159-171.

Zovanyi, G. 2005. Urban growth management and ecological sustainability: confronting the "smart growth" fallacy. In: Bengston, D.N., tech. ed. Policies for managing urban growth and landscape change: a key to conservation in the 21st century. Gen. Tech. Rep. NC-265. St. Paul, MN: U.S. Department of Agriculture, Forest Service, North Central Research Station: 35-44.

Urban Growth Management and Ecological Sustainability: Confronting the "Smart Growth" Fallacy

Gabor Zovanyi[1]

ABSTRACT—Growth management and Smart Growth initiatives in the United States represent an ongoing process of growth accommodation. Because growth by definition constitutes unsustainable behavior in that it is incapable of being continued or maintained indefinitely, ongoing growth accommodation must be recognized as activity incongruous with advancing the goal of ecological sustainability. This paper portrays the growth-accommodation practices that make up growth management and Smart Growth initiatives today; considers the magnitudes of ongoing demographic, economic, and urban growth destined to nullify those initiatives; and suggests alternative growth management endeavors to further ecological sustainability.

GROWTH MANAGEMENT IN THE UNITED STATES

A growth management movement emerged in the United States during the late 1960s and early 1970s in response to an ideological shift in public perceptions about the value of further growth (Reilly 1973, Scott 1975). During this period the traditional association of population, economic, and urban growth with societal progress gave way to a new and more skeptical view that associated growth with problems like overcrowded schools, tax increases, rising crime rates, physical blight, traffic congestion, loss of open space, and increasing air and water pollution. This ideological shift in American attitudes toward growth came to affect popular perceptions about the development of land, because uses of land also were linked to a number of specific problems during this period. Growth, as manifested in the development of land, was blamed for such diverse problems as the costly and destructive development pattern associated with urban sprawl, loss of prime agricultural land, an inefficient provision of public facilities and services, escalating housing prices, pervasive environmental degradation, and loss of community character. Growth management was advanced as an avenue for addressing these ills associated with future growth and its accompanying land development without having to repudiate growth.

Proponents of growth management responded to the new perception that growth had to be managed, regulated, or controlled, rather than simply promoted as in the past, by proposing *management* strategies for addressing problems attributed to growth. It was suggested, for example, that containing growth within designated urban growth boundaries would hold down the cost of providing public facilities and services, while conserving rural resource lands and protecting environmentally sensitive lands from sprawling development. Although growth-management literature distinguishes between *growth management* and *growth control* (Landis 1992, Levy 1994)—the former is associated with attempts to influence the *location* or *quality* of growth and the latter is associated with efforts to limit the *amount* or *rate* of growth—research has revealed a strong bias in favor of *management* over *control* (Finkler and Peterson 1974, Glickfeld and Levine 1991). In fact, the overwhelming majority of local growth management programs implemented to date clearly reflect continued growth accommodation practices rather than the imposition of limits (Zovanyi 1998). These management programs have not sought to reduce either the overall *amount* or the *rate* of growth. They have instead reflected the belief that growth can continue to be accommodated if its *location* is properly planned and its *quality* ensured by providing adequate infrastructure and mitigating negative effects.

Although local governments have been the principal players in implementing growth management programs in the United States, some states have passed laws asserting a state role in growth management activities (DeGrove and Miness 1992, Zovanyi 1998). To date, 11 states have passed statewide laws giving direction to growth management actions in local communities, and these laws have uniformly reinforced the noted growth-accommodation orientation of local programs. All these statewide laws contain provisions intended to promote ongoing growth, and in 8 of the 11 states, the laws actually mandate ongoing growth accommodation by local governments (Zovanyi 1999). In Washington state, for example, local governments are required to adjust their urban growth boundaries every 10 years to accommodate the next 20 years of state-projected growth. However, local communities have shown a bias in favor of such accommodative management programs even in states like California where they have operated in the absence of statewide laws directing their management activities. As growth management advocates have acknowledged: "Growth management systems are inherently growth-accommodating" (Nelson and Duncan 1995: 111).

[1] Department of Urban Planning, Health and Public Administration, Eastern Washington University, 668 N. Riverpoint Blvd., Spokane, WA 99202-1660; e-mail: gzovanyi@mail.ewu.edu

Citation for proceedings: Bengston, David N., tech. ed. 2005. Policies for managing urban growth and landscape change: a key to conservation in the 21st Century. Gen. Tech. Rep. NC-265. St. Paul, MN: U.S. Department of Agriculture, Forest Service, North Central Research Station. 51 p.

The Pro-Growth Bias of Growth Management

The growth-accommodation orientation of growth management in America may be attributed to the strong pro-growth bias that permeates the management movement. That pro-growth bias is evident in growth management literature. Those who have written on the subject have affixed a number of modifiers to the word growth to justify its continuance and have in the process revealed their pro-growth inclinations. Their writings refer to "inevitable, normal, reasonable, proper, realistic, sensible, responsible, and legitimate" growth (Zovanyi 1998). These spokespersons for the growth management movement also refer to "balanced growth," arguing that a balance can be achieved between the equally legitimate ends of ongoing growth and environmental protection without compromising either (DeGrove 1989). As the growth management movement evolved, it became fashionable to refer to "smart growth" as an alternative to the "dumb growth" represented by sprawl (Chen 2000, Lorentz and Shaw 2000), a distinction that suggested the problem was not with growth per se but rather its inefficient manifestation in the form of sprawl. Representatives of the management movement even suggest the possibility of "sustainable growth" (Kaiser *et al.* 1995: 172, Nelson and Duncan 1995: xi), when growth in the material terms represented by demographic, economic, and urban increases is by definition unsustainable because it cannot be maintained or continued indefinitely. In the end, a case can be made for the claim that the pro-growth bias demonstrated by those in the growth management movement has translated into an institutionalized form of support for the growth imperative that pervades all aspects of American culture (Zovanyi 1999, 2000).

The Absence of Sustainability Considerations in Growth Management

Growth management in the United States has shown little regard for sustainability since the movement began in the late 1960s and early 1970s (Zovanyi 1998). The absence of such considerations during the 1970s and 1980s is understandable, because interest in sustainable development in the United States did not emerge until the 1990s. However, the continued dearth of concern about sustainability in growth management during the 1990s and the current decade is more difficult to explain in light of the global interest in sustainable development during that period. Part of the explanation undoubtedly stems from the complexity of any formulation of sustainable development and the resultant difficulty of incorporating such a formulation into specific growth management programs. The sustainable development movement postulates that a sustainable society must balance social equity, economic prosperity, and environmental integrity (Krizek and Power 1996), and addressing all these "3 Es" of sustainability would require growth management initiatives to simultaneously confront "social sustainability," "economic sustainability," and "environmental sustainability." The challenges associated with advancing such an agenda might therefore be assumed to explain at least part of the failure of the growth management movement to incorporate sustainability.

Another plausible explanation for the paucity of sustainability concerns in growth management initiatives to date is the conundrum presented by the irreconcilable incongruity between growth and sustainability. Growth does not satisfy what has been referred to as the distinguishing characteristic of sustainability, which is the ability to be continued or maintained (Shearman 1990). Because the growth management movement is committed to the virtue of ongoing growth, the impossibility of reconciling continued growth with sustainable behavior also might be offered as a partial explanation of why the growth management movement has largely ignored the matter of sustainability to date. However, many current formulations of sustainable development assume there are prospects for further growth if it is merely the right kind, i.e., growth based on an efficient use of materials and energy. This viewpoint leads to optimism about the possibility of realizing greater economic prosperity, as one of the noted dimensions of sustainable development, via continued economic growth without jeopardizing the quest for sustainability. These suggested prospects for "sustainable growth" have not, however, been adopted as a component of the pro-growth rationale employed by members of the growth management movement.

Sustainable development literature in America addresses the need to limit sprawl, create compact communities, revitalize existing urban centers, preserve natural ecosystems, and reduce resource use, pollution, and automobile use (Beatley and Manning 1997, Wheeler 2000). Sustainable communities literature in the United States, in turn, tends to make a case for more compact and contiguous development patterns, reduced automobile dependency and alternative forms of transportation, mixed-use developments and infill growth, and reduced resource consumption and waste generation (Breheny and Rockwood 1993, Van der Ryan and Calthorpe 1986). As it turns out, traditional growth management and its current manifestation in the form of a Smart Growth movement both have a lot in common with these stated aims. Proponents of Smart Growth, as the following section will reveal, also favor limiting sprawl; creating compact, mixed-use communities; curtailing automobile use; and supporting infill development over outlying development. However, these similar ends have been justified by different rationales from those used by sustainable development and sustainable communities advocates. For Smart Growth proponents the primary rationale for containing sprawl and promoting compact settlements has been one of avoiding costly and inefficient facility and service provisions across the landscape. Among sustainable development and sustainable communities advocates, the primary rationale has rather been one of pursuing prospective reductions in resource consumption and waste generation. When Smart Growth proponents advocate containment of growth as a way of reducing the loss of agricultural and forestry resource lands, they have not based their concern on a desire to achieve a sustainable use of such resources in the manner of those in the sustainability camps, but rather on a desire to avoid declines in resource-based sectors of state economies. However, these differences belie a striking similarity among the three groups: all share a decidedly pro-growth bias (Zovanyi 2004). All three camps continue to espouse the possibility of transforming ongoing growth into a socially and environmentally benign form of expansion.

Few communities have undertaken sustainable development initiatives in the United States, and their efforts have not been linked to growth management programs. Those initiatives have typically focused on tracking sets of sustainability indicators to measure movement toward or away from sustainability in various areas (Krizek and Power 1996). Although these efforts have drawn on former work in tracking quality-of-life indicators in American communities, sustainability indicators have expanded the inquiry in environmental and ecological terms not evident in earlier attempts to track a community's quality of life. Earlier sets of quality-of-life indicators tended to emphasize anthropocentric social and economic considerations at the expense of environmental and ecological matters, as typified by the highly publicized case of Jacksonville, Florida which devoted only 10 percent of its 80 indicators to environmental and ecological concerns. Sustainability indicators, on the other hand, have tended to reveal a greater balance across social, economic, and environmental indicators due to the noted belief among sustainability advocates that true sustainability advances require a balanced pursuit of social, economic, and environmental sustainability. For example, 34 percent and 38 percent of the sustainability indicators in Burlington, Vermont, and Santa Monica, California are devoted to environmental considerations, respectively. Because sustainability indicators are less likely to shortchange environmental and ecological considerations than quality-of-life indicators, any incorporation of sustainability indicators into growth management initiatives might have enhanced the prospects of growth management addressing the critical matter of ecological sustainability. After all, "sustainability is at bottom *an ecological concept*" (Worster 1993: 148) and, as ecologists are apt to note, without ecological sustainability no other forms of sustainability will be possible. Sadly, spokespersons for the growth management movement have yet to acknowledge this truism, and as a result the movement has paid little attention to sustainability indicators, sustainability in general, or the critical matter of ecological sustainability in particular (Zovanyi 1998).

SMART GROWTH INITIATIVES IN THE UNITED STATES

By the 1990s growth management in America had evolved to encompass additional concerns and in the process had adopted the nomenclature of Smart Growth. This new Smart Growth movement has maintained an allegiance to the "efficiency" and "anti-sprawl" commitments demonstrated by growth management initiatives during the 1970s and 1980s. As noted in one growth management text: "Growth management is intimately associated with the achievement of more efficient urban development patterns" (Nelson and Duncan 1995: 12). This efficiency theme appears repeatedly in Smart Growth writings. Some observers have suggested that using land more efficiently constitutes a basic principle of Smart Growth (Avin and Holden 2000). A document produced by the American Planning Association identified the efficient use of land resources as one of six principles of smart development (APA 1998). Another commentator noted: "*Smart Growth* refers to development principles and planning practices that create more efficient land use and transport patterns" (Litman 2003: 2). Yet other observers contended: "The panoply of

smart growth strategies includes many things, but at its core it seeks to use an area's land resources—both urbanized and raw—as efficiently as possible" (Danielsen *et al.* 1999: 12).

Smart Growth publications reveal as much of a commitment to an anti-sprawl stance as the prior commitment to efficiency in the use of land resources, which is to be expected because realizing efficiency in those terms is assumed to depend on reining in sprawl. Such a growth containment commitment to combat sprawl was a characteristic feature of earlier growth management initiatives, and the anti-sprawl bias continues to be demonstrated in Smart Growth writings. This anti-sprawl bias has been reinforced by general public opposition to sprawl, as revealed by a 2000 Pew Center opinion poll that found that of all local issues, such as crime, jobs, and education, Americans were most worried about sprawl and traffic. In that year the pace of land development, according to the U.S. Department of Agriculture, was roughly double what it was a decade earlier (Chen 2000), which compounded problems like traffic congestion and the loss of open space, and produced an interest in Smart Growth as an alternative to sprawl (Lorentz and Shaw 2000). One assessment of Smart Growth concluded: "Proponents of smart growth tout its more compact, less automobile dependent development as a superior alternative to the prevailing pattern of sprawl" (Burchell *et al.* 2000: 821). According to other analysts: "'Smart growth' is a term used to describe efforts to shape growth in a way that lessens sprawl" (Danielsen *et al.* 1999: 12). In the words of yet another observer: "Throughout the U.S., the term 'smart growth' is being adopted by groups trying to change what they regard as the undesirable impacts of 'suburban sprawl'" (Downs 2001: 20). But Smart Growth encompasses much more than a quest to realize more efficient land use patterns through the curtailment of sprawl; it also embodies a range of other sought after ends that analysts have attempted to summarize via a set of Smart Growth principles.

There have been multiple attempts to portray the tenets of Smart Growth, with contributors identifying anywhere from 5 to 14 Smart Growth principles (APA 1998, Benfield *et al.* 1999, Burchell *et al.* 2000, Downs 2001, Litman 2003, Porter 2002, Smart-Growth Network 2002). The various principles identified by these analysts may be grouped into five categories that represent the major tenets of Smart Growth: growth containment; compact, mixed-use development; multimodal transportation; protection of open space, resource lands, and the environment; and collaborative planning and decisionmaking. Except for the focus on design innovations in the "compact, mixed-use development" principle, aspects of the other four principles have been addressed by the growth management movement since its inception.

The principle of growth containment has found expression in an ongoing emphasis on urban growth boundaries to contain growth within urban growth areas. This containment of growth within designated growth areas has been considered critical to curtailing sprawl and achieving greater efficiencies in land use and transportation patterns. Growth containment has also been advocated on grounds of realizing greater efficiencies in providing public infrastructure and services. The resulting emphasis on infill development, including the use of so-called brownfield sites in cities and suburbs, over development at the urban/suburban periphery, on so-called greenfield sites, also has been championed because it supports the revitalization of long-neglected older communities in desperate need of redevelopment. And finally, the growth containment principle has been championed because of its connection to the protection of open space, resource lands, and the environment principle. In this regard, proponents of growth management argue that concentrated development is essential to realizing the ends of open space preservation, resource lands conservation, and environmental protection of sensitive lands in outlying areas.

With respect to the multi-model transportation principle, growth management advocates have made the case against low-density, dispersed, automobile-dependent sprawl since the earliest days of the movement. They argued the case for an alternative land use pattern that would provide expanded mobility via transportation options. The early emphasis tended to center on containing growth at sufficient densities to support public transit. Over time attention shifted to "accessibility" and "connectivity," and the creation of land use patterns that would support walking and cycling in addition to options for transit and a declining emphasis on automobiles. The collaborative planning and decision making principle of Smart Growth also has undergone changes as the growth management movement has evolved. Initially, spokespersons for the movement made the case for the need to simplify the complex and time-consuming process of obtaining development approval. This call for streamlining permitting procedures for development in keeping with growth management aims was seen as a necessary and responsible antidote to the growing opposition to all development irrespective of whether it represented "dumb growth" or "smart growth." During the more recent Smart Growth era, the call has continued for streamlined review and faster project approval under a predictable, fair, and cost-effective development review process, but the collaborative planning and decisionmaking principle also has called for an inclusive decisionmaking process encompassing all stakeholders and a public-private, consensus-building process intended to achieve far more than an expedited development approval process.

Because the prior review of Smart Growth principles reveals some change in growth management concerns over time, the most significant changes have resulted from the design innovations embodied within the compact, mixed-use development principle. Although this principle only started to affect growth management practices during the Smart Growth era that began in the mid-1990s, its design elements are clearly drawn from the past and serve to promote development reminiscent of an earlier time in America. The design nomenclature of Smart Growth, which is alternatively represented by the terms "neo-traditionalism," "traditional neighborhood development," or "new urbanism," is inspired by a nostalgic view of "community" that was perceived to exist in American villages, towns, and urban neighborhoods during the early decades of the 20th century. The enclaves that housed such community were characterized by compact, mixed-use development, higher densities that enhanced "walkability" and supported public transit, and active community life. These compact enclaves, typically

defined by a radius of no more than a quarter of a mile, and containing a rich mix of residential and nonresidential uses, are credited with enhancing livability in a number of ways. Their human scale is said to promote access for pedestrians and bicycles, thereby reducing automobile usage. Their density is believed to create diverse options for housing, including affordable housing. Their emphasis on public spaces, such as pedestrian areas and parks, over private spaces, such as yards, gated communities, and clubs, is assumed to enhance citizen interaction and thereby achieve community identity and a sense of space. Yet other design features, such as front porches and modified street grid patterns that accommodate a variety of activities, are similarly believed to enhance neighborhood ambiance and contribute to a sense of community. All these perceived benefits have created such support for the relevance of new urbanism in the design of new developments that in the minds of many it has become equated with Smart Growth.

The most controversial aspect of the design innovations embodied in the new urbanism view of Smart Growth has undoubtedly been the call for higher densities in future developments. While growth management traditionally implied higher densities associated with the containment of growth within urban growth areas, the design emphasis of new urbanism that many equate with Smart Growth has upped the ante by calling for even higher densities within compact enclaves of development wherever they occur on the landscape, whether in urban, suburban, or exurban settings (Litman 2003: 7). Within urban settings these higher-density centers have come to be referred to as "nodes" in a "nodes and corridors" development scheme in which the higher density nodes are linked by corridors of public transit. The higher densities within both urban growth areas and their multiple, compact, mixed-use nodes are seen as essential to realizing efficiencies in land use that will permit ongoing growth accommodation without defeating other growth management ends such as conserving resource lands and protecting environmentally sensitive lands outside urban centers. Land savings associated with compact, higher density development may be illustrated by pointing out that it would take 1,000 acres to accommodate 1,000 dwelling units at 1 unit per acre, only 167 acres to accommodate those 1,000 units in townhouses built at 6 units per acre, and a mere 83 acres to accommodate the same 1,000 units at 12 units per acre in mixed-use buildings housing a couple of stories of residential units above ground-level commercial uses. Proponents of Smart Growth see prospects for endless growth accommodation under such efficient use of land, and this perspective allows them to maintain their allegiance to the growth imperative in a fashion that characterizes the entire history of the growth management movement in America. Advocates of Smart Growth have been unwilling to acknowledge that ongoing growth would inevitably nullify any short-term savings in the amount of land consumed by development and have instead continued to exhibit an optimistic, pro-growth bias.

The Pro-Growth Bias of Smart Growth Initiatives

Literature addressing the current Smart Growth avenue of growth management shows a decidedly pro-growth bias in keeping with the growth orientation of more traditional management theory and practice. That literature reveals the same traditional view of the supposed "inevitability" of growth: "Smart growth advocates argue that while growth is inevitable, sprawl is not" (Danielsen *et al.* 1999: 12). The literature also reflects the growth accommodation orientation of earlier management writings: "A basic principle of smart growth should be to accommodate future growth, not choke it off" (Downs 2001: 25). According to another commentator, "smart growth means development that accommodates growth in smart ways" (Porter 2002: 1). That same commentator also illustrated the Smart Growth movement's pro-growth orientation in the following direct terms: "Smart growth offers a 21st-century, pro-growth path to creating livable communities" (Porter 2002: 2). The historical pro-growth bias of growth management in the United States has therefore been reinforced rather than modified during the more recent Smart Growth management era.

The Sustainability Void in Smart Growth Programs

In addition to contributing nothing to a possible reassessment of the growth management movement's pro-growth orientation, the Smart Growth movement has done little to advance sustainability concerns within growth management. Smart Growth literature does give lip service to sustainability, as in the expressed view that "a future...with smarter growth will be more prosperous as well as more environmentally sustainable and socially equitable" (Benfield *et al.* 1999: 2). The literature even claims that "Many sustainable development aims are reflected in smart-growth principles" (Porter 2002: 5). In reality, however, Smart Growth programs have largely ignored the early sustainable development focus on conserving and recycling natural resources, and to date they have paid scant attention to the current sustainable development emphasis on interrelating and balancing economic prosperity, the integrity of natural ecosystems, and social equity. Although Smart Growth literature shows some overlap with sustainable development and sustainable communities literature, in that writings in all three areas advocate compact development and reduced automobile dependency, the Smart Growth movement has demonstrated virtually no commitment to sustainability such as reducing resource consumption and waste generation or preserving natural ecosystems. The movement has not therefore moved growth management toward a greater regard for sustainability in general or ecological sustainability in particular.

ACKNOWLEDGING CURRENT GROWTH CHALLENGES

Past growth management and its current manifestation in the form of Smart Growth practices have both tended to focus on growth management strategies and techniques, with little if any regard for the magnitudes of demographic, economic, and urban growth to be managed. The rapid growth experienced during the past 50 years internationally and nationally has been accepted as a given within the management movement, rather than as something to be debated or questioned. The movement has demonstrated no awareness that more people have been added to the world's population in the last 50 years than in all the prior history of our species (Brown 2001: 19). It also has shown no interest in the fact that "growth in the

world economy during the year 2000 exceeded that during the entire nineteenth century" (Brown 2001: 19). Nor has the management movement addressed the reality of urban growth rates exceeding demographic and economic growth rates globally, resulting in a projected doubling of the number of people living in cities to 5 billion between 1990 and 2025 (Hall and Pfeiffer 2000) and increasing the number of megacities of over 8 million from only 2 in 1950 to 21 in 1990 and an expected 33 in 2015 (World Resources Institute 1996). Any consideration of these dramatic increases might be expected to result in a questioning of the merit of a continued pro-growth bias in any geographical context, but the growth management movement has ignored the magnitudes being generated by growth globally as well as nationally.

Demographic Growth in the United States

Unsustainable demographic growth has certainly been demonstrated in America during the recent past. The 1990s set a record for the number of people added to the United States in a single decade, with the 33 million increase of that decade surpassing the 28 million added during the post-war, baby-boom decade of the 1950s. That growth rate, which translates into the addition of another 3.3 million individuals each year, may in growth management terms be thought of as representing the equivalent of 33 cities of 100,000 every 12 months to accommodate the increase. The wisdom of assuming that Smart Growth will make it possible to sustain these annual increases would certainly be questioned by some within the growth management movement if participants addressed and debated the numbers.

Economic Growth in the United States

Economic growth in the United States has recently rebounded from a national recession, and the wisdom of the resultant economic magnitudes being generated might also be questioned by growth-management proponents if management debates were ever to consider these numbers. The 7.2 percent economic growth rate experienced during the third quarter of 2003 would double the already enormous size of the American economy in a mere 10 years. Ten such doublings in a century under that rate of growth would yield an economy 1 thousand times larger, and another 10 doublings during a second century would expand the economy to 1 million times its present size. Admittedly, most economists do not expect a 7 percent growth rate to continue and instead speak of economic growth between 2 and 3 percent as a level capable of being "sustained." A projected rate of 4.6 percent was announced for 2004, which represents a doubling time of some 15 years. Any of these rates would yield the same absurd outcome produced by the 7 percent growth rate, generating a national economy a million times larger than the current level; it would merely take longer to reach that level under lower growth rates. In this regard proponents of growth management appear to side with neoclassical growth economists in believing that economic growth can be continued indefinitely if it is smart growth, which for economists translates into growth based on an efficient use of resources and energy. Both groups seem unwilling to consider that ongoing growth will nullify any such efficiency savings, as in the case of a 50 percent reduction in resource use or pollution generation being negated by a subsequent doubling of the economy.

Urban Growth in the United States

The magnitude of urban growth in the recent past may be illustrated by research that has documented the conversion of rural land to developed uses under ongoing urbanization and development over the past two decades. That research, conducted by the U.S. Department of Agriculture's Natural Resources Conservation Service, released in a 2001 report indicated about 34 million acres of rural land were converted to developed uses between 1982 and 2001 (U.S. Department of Agriculture, NRCS 2001). This represented the conversion of a total area about the size of Illinois over that period or the equivalent of the conversion of an area roughly the size of Vermont every 3 years. That same report pointed out that the rate of development was escalating, averaging 2.2 million acres per year during the 1990s, as opposed to 1.4 million acres per year during the 1980s. Recent research has disclosed that for the 100 largest urbanized areas in America about half of the conversion is attributable to the increase in the number of residents in those areas, while the other half is attributable to an increase in the average amount of land consumed per resident (Kolankiewicz and Beck 2001).

It also has been pointed out that most of America's metropolitan areas are adding urbanized land at a much faster rate than they are adding population. Nationwide the amount of urbanized land increased by 47 percent between 1982 and 1997, whereas the nation's population grew by only 17 percent during that period (Porter 2002: 29). These figures clearly point to a decline in densities over time in America's urbanized areas. It has been calculated that in 1920 the average density of all urbanized areas was 6,160 persons per square mile, or a little less than 10 persons per acre. By 1990 that figure had declined by over half to 2,589 persons per square mile, or about 4 persons per acre. Most striking, however, is that developments built since 1960 only average about 1,469 persons per square mile, or a little over 2 persons per acre (Benfield et al. 1999: 12). The Smart Growth response is urban containment with higher densities as a way of reducing the amount of land converted from rural to urban uses. Again, proponents of this strategy ignore the fact that ongoing growth will negate such savings, as in a case where the land consumption associated with 1,000 new residents would be cut in half only to have those land savings nullified by the next allotment of 1,000 new residents. The noted magnitudes of demographic, economic, and urban increases recently generated by growth are clearly incapable of being sustained indefinitely, so any short-term support for such increases must be based on the belief that there are no existent limits to growth. That belief is being challenged by mounting evidence that these limits have already been reached and surpassed.

GROWTH MANAGEMENT IN AN ERA OF EXISTENT LIMITS TO GROWTH

In 1972 the book *Limits to Growth* presented the incontrovertible axiom that infinite growth is impossible in a finite system, and based on the findings of computer modeling predicted that global limits to growth would be reached within 100 years (Meadows et al. 1972). The 1992 sequel to that book, *Beyond the Limits*, claimed that some of those limits had already been reached, as reflected by unsustainable resource use and pollution generation (Meadows et al. 1992). Other research findings reported during the 1990s supported the claim of existent limits to growth.

Global Limits to Growth

During the early 1990s the case for existent limits to growth was made on multiple grounds, including the destruction of renewable resources (Ehrlich and Ehrlich 1990), pervasive environmental constraints (Brown et al. 1994), loss of essential ecological life-support services (Ehrlich and Ehrlich 1991), anthropogenic climate change (Goodland 1992), lost ground in feeding an expanding global population (Brown and Kane 1994), and declining biodiversity (Wilson 1992). Reported findings such as these led to the conclusion that we had already exceeded the planet's carrying capacity before the close of the 20th century: "As a result of our population size, consumption patterns, and technology choices, we have surpassed the planet's carrying capacity" (Postel 1994: 40). The current decade has reinforced the view of surpassed limits with new findings. Ocean-related research revealed the percentage of the world's coral reefs that were severely damaged had increased from 10 to 27 percent between 1992 and 2000 (Mastny 2002), and commercial fishing had already eliminated at least 90 percent of all large ocean predators such as sharks by 2003 (Myers and Worm 2003).

The impact of an expanding human enterprise on ecosystems worldwide may be illustrated by the threats currently posed to other species by the present size of that enterprise. In 2002 the World Conservation Union reported that worldwide 25 percent of mammals, 12 percent of birds, 25 percent of reptiles, 21 percent of amphibians, and 30 percent of fish were already threatened with extinction (World Conservation Union 2002). Noted ecologists have warned that under current and accelerating trends fully 50 percent of the remaining species on the planet could be eliminated by 2050 (Ehrlich and Ehrlich 1991: 34, Wilson 1992: 278). As the scale of the human enterprise grows exponentially, ecosystems succumb to that expansion and the planet's biodiversity is being subjected to an assault that has been referred to as "biological meltdown" (Manes 1990). Conservation biologists agree the principal cause of biodiversity decline is habitat loss as expanding human activities eliminate ecosystems. The reality of declining biodiversity may be taken as further evidence humans have exceeded the planet's carrying capacity.

A case for existent limits to growth has additionally been based on the findings of ecological footprint analyses. Those analyses determine the total area of land and water required to produce the resources that a given population consumes and assimilate the wastes it generates, wherever on Earth that land and water is located. A recent assessment of the per capita footprint of humans globally revealed an average ecological footprint of some 5.7 acres, whereas the planet was found to contain only about 4.2 acres of biotically productive space per capita, resulting in a global deficit of 1.5 acres per capita (Wackernagel et al. 1997). These calculations reveal the current ecological footprint of humanity already exceeds the planet's ecological capacity to sustain the present size of the human enterprise. Rather than living off the annual renewable productive capacity or "income" of renewable resources, humans are already consuming the "capital" base of those resources, which is further evidence of existent global limits to growth.

Limits to Growth in the United States

As early as 1982 research in America indicated the levels of population and economic activity of that period were damaging and depleting the nation's natural capital across a range of renewable resources (Webb and Jacobsen 1982). As elsewhere on the planet, Americans during that period were consuming the capital base of renewable resources, rather than living off their annual renewable productive capacity. Even then that behavior was translating into diminished fertility on agricultural lands, overgrazed grasslands, overharvested fisheries, depleted groundwater supplies, and truncated natural forests, which indicated the country was already experiencing existent limits to growth.

By the 1990s nationwide research on the prior loss of ecosystems in America provided further evidence that the country had already surpassed national limits to growth (Noss *et al.* 1997). That research concluded 27 ecosystem types had declined by an alarming 98 percent or more since European settlement of North America. The ongoing degradation and destruction of ecosystems and the habitats they represent is the leading cause of declining biodiversity in American as it is elsewhere on the planet. A comprehensive assessment undertaken in 1997 of some 20 thousand species of plants and animals native to the United States revealed fully a third were "of conservation concern," i.e., believed to be extinct, imperiled, or vulnerable (The Nature Conservancy 1997). The matter of habitat loss and its contribution to declining biodiversity is an issue not only in rural areas subjected to the pressures of ongoing urban expansion, but also in America's cities and suburbs. For example, habitats are lost as infill development eliminates urban and suburban forests that are logged to make way for more growth. The American Forests organization has been researching this phenomenon for more than 20 years, and its analyses have revealed dramatic declines in tree cover across American communities. A 2002 analysis of San Antonio covering the period from 1985 to 2001 discovered a 39 percent decline in the city's heavy tree cover (areas with greater than 50 percent canopy) (American Forests 2002), and a 2003 analysis of San Diego revealed a loss of 27 percent of its tree cover between 1985 and 2002 (American Forests 2003). The organization's work in the Puget Sound, Atlanta, and Chesapeake Bay regions revealed the heavy tree canopy in all those areas has declined by more than one-third in just 25 years.

Ecological footprint analyses also suggest existent limits to growth in the United States. Such research has concluded that the average American has an ecological footprint of more than 20 acres (Wackernagel and Yount 1998), which is more than 5 times the available per capita allotment of 4.2 acres of biotically productive space on a worldwide basis. Americans are only able to generate such enormous footprints by exceeding their own national ecological capacity and running national ecological deficits with other countries. These figures suggest the planet would have to be five times its present size to support the ecological load of the Earth's six billion people living American lifestyles. Rather than taking actions to moderate

their per capita ecological footprints, Americans have continued to increase their footprints over recent decades. New development for decades has demonstrated "a rise in the amount of land claimed per household" (Benfield *et al.* 1999: 13). "According to the U.S. Census, the median size of a new single-family home rose 39 percent in the last twenty years—from 1,520 square feet in 1982 to 2,114 square feet in 2002" (Gann 2004: 5). Vehicles have gotten larger and fuel efficiency has declined since 1987 (Brown 2001: 101; Sawin 2004: 29), and vehicle miles traveled per capita have gone up from 3,979 miles in 1960 to 9,220 in 1995 (Benfield: 1999: 32). Instead of transitioning to a more sustainable relationship with the natural world during prior decades in response to new ecological realities, Americans have gravitated to a less sustainable position.

ECOLOGICAL SUSTAINABILITY AS THE NEW GROWTH MANAGEMENT FOCUS

The exponential expansion of the human enterprise over the course of the past 50 years has put humankind in a troubled relationship with the natural world. In 1991 the Ecological Society of America declared the existing scale of the human enterprise was "threatening the sustainability of Earth's life-support systems" (Lubchenco *et al.* 1991: 377). In 2002 an international team of ecologists, economists, and conservation biologists published a study indicating that nearly all ecosystems on the planet are shrinking in response to expanding human demands on the natural world (Balmford *et al.* 2002). Similar findings of global ecological decline are revealed by the Living Planet Index, which measures changes in forest, freshwater, and marine ecosystems, and which recently recorded a 37-percent decline in the planet's ecological health in these terms since 1970 (WWF International 2002). Ecosystems and the services they provide are under assault because the expanding scale of human activities is displacing the natural landscapes that make up ecosystems. Prior exponential growth of the human enterprise and its associated destruction and degradation of ecosystems worldwide have already "brought the world to the brink of ecological disaster" (Ehrlich and Ehrlich 1991: 285).

The human enterprise is supported by ecosystem services that provide the very foundation of the civilization fashioned from those services. Growth in demographic, economic, and urban terms is now degrading the ecological life-support services needed to sustain humankind. These forms of physical growth are responsible for the ongoing destruction and degradation of ecosystems and the associated loss of biodiversity. As long as the growth imperative driving current cultural behavior spins off population, economic, and urban growth at exponential rates, it will displace natural ecosystems at exponential rates and in turn push the number of extinctions to increase exponentially. It is time to recognize that the growth imperative driving continued growth has now become an obsolete and lethal ideology, and that humankind must abandon the growth imperative if it is to experience an indeterminate future. It must be acknowledged that our species can exist without growth, but not without sustainable ecosystems. Current ecological realities dictate that the growth imperative driving current human behavior must be replaced with the imperative of ecological sustainability. There is an urgent need to base the quest for a sustainable future on the primacy of ecological sustainability. Since civilization is utterly dependent upon sound ecosystems that are threatened by ongoing growth, that growth must be terminated and ecological sustainability must become the new primary focus of both society at large and the current Smart Growth version of growth management.

Confronting the Smart Growth Fallacy

At present the growth management movement in the United States and its current manifestation in the form of the Smart Growth movement are impeding the essential transition from the growth imperative to an ecological imperative. Both growth management and Smart Growth advocates remain committed to the assumed wisdom of future growth. They argue that negative growth effects can be mitigated sufficiently to permit continued growth, in effect suggesting that ongoing growth can be transformed into a form of socially and environmentally benign expansion. They even condemn the idea that management activities might legitimately be directed at efforts to stop growth, asserting this would represent inefficient, unjust, and irresponsible behavior. The growth management movement remains wedded to growth accommodation practices.

Mere management of ongoing growth must be acknowledged to be an insufficient response to the ecological realities of the early 21st century. The fact that even the present size of the human enterprise is degrading the ecosystems that sustain humankind and driving other species to extinction ought to be ample proof that further growth constitutes irresponsible behavior. Instead of conceding this fact, management proponents continue to defend the ideas of balanced growth, smart growth, and even sustainable growth at a time when growth-induced ecological problems increasingly demonstrate the irresponsible nature of ongoing growth accommodation practices. It is possible to think of this pro-growth stance in terms of a growth management delusion (Zovanyi 1999), with the delusion that it will be possible to protect the environment under ongoing growth. Psychiatrists define delusion as a false, persistent belief maintained in spite of evidence to the contrary. The growth management movement represents continued support of ongoing growth in spite of mounting evidence that growth no longer represents a viable policy option or survival strategy. A point has been reached in human history where further population, economic, and urban growth must be rejected if humankind is to preserve the ecosystems and biodiversity that sustain the human enterprise.

Neither traditional growth management nor current Smart Growth advocates have shown any willingness to address sustainability concerns in general or ecological sustainability considerations in particular, and have instead focused on what they consider to be responsible accommodation of inevitable growth. This myopic perspective allows them to advance a Smart Growth fallacy, i.e., the false or mistaken idea of the possibility of sustainable growth. Growth in demographic, economic, or urban terms does not represent sustainable behavior. No amount of wishful thinking or elaborate management practices will make growth sustainable in these terms. In the end, Smart Growth is just as unsustainable as dumb growth, and over time will eventually produce the same intolerable conditions.

The No-Growth Option for Growth Management

The community plans and land use regulations produced as part of current growth management and Smart Growth initiatives typically embody prospects for absurd levels of future growth accommodation. A statewide analysis of the plans and regulations in the growth management state of Florida illustrates the point. A 1999 report revealed city and county plans and associated land use controls would permit the state to grow from its then 15 million people to over 100 million under development based on the highest density permitted by those documents (Howard 1999). Most of America's cities and counties also are vastly overzoned and overplatted. Their existing zoning districts and previously approved subdivisions of land represent enormous unrealized capacity for future land development. Current growth management and Smart Growth initiatives only increase that development capacity. These ridiculous prospects for future growth must be recognized as representing unsustainable futures for America's communities. It must also be conceded that Smart Growth will at best only slow the process of ecological decay under more efficient utilization of land, instead of advancing true ecological sustainability.

A number of strategies are available to local governments for initiating a transition to a state of nongrowth, and a case may be made for the claim that such strategies would be capable of surviving legal challenges (Zovanyi 2000). Communities could, for example, modify their comprehensive land use plans and land use regulations to reflect a research-based cap on growth, e.g., documenting that available water supplies are insufficient to support ongoing growth. They could terminate public investments in capital facility programs that make ongoing growth possible. They could also create a permanent urban growth boundary to physically limit further growth in the form of sprawl. Additionally, they could take private land out of development by acquiring it and holding it in public trust. And finally, they could act to stop the job formation that fuels further growth. The alternative to these sorts of strategies is a continuation of the unsustainable growth accommodation practices of current growth management and Smart Growth initiatives in America. Existent ecological realities call out for alternative management practices based on the primary sustainability consideration of ecological sustainability.

LITERATURE CITED

American Forests. 2002. Urban ecosystem analysis, San Antonio, TX. Washington, DC: American Forests. 8 p. [Available online: http://www.americanforests.org]

American Forests. 2003. Urban ecosystem analysis, San Diego, CA. Washington, DC: American Forests. 20 p. [Available online: http://www.americanforests.org]

American Planning Association. 1998. The principles of smart development. Chicago, IL: American Planning Association. 108 p.

Avin, U.P.; Holden, D.R. 2000. Does your growth smart? Planning. 66(1): 26-29.

Balmford, L. *et al.* 2002. Economic reasons for conserving wild nature. Science. 9(2): 27-39.

Beatley, T.; Manning, K. 1997. The ecology of place: planning for environment, economy, and community. Washington, DC: Island Press. 265 p.

Benfield, F.K.; Raimi, M.D.; Chen, D.D.T. 1999. Once there were greenfields: how urban sprawl is undermining America's environment, economy, and social fabric. Washington, DC: Natural Resources Defense Council. 215 p.

Breheny, M.; Rockwood, R. 1993. Planning the sustainable city region. In: Blowers, A., ed. Planning for a sustainable environment: a report by the town and country planning association. London, England: Earthscan Publications, Ltd.: 42-63.

Brown, L.R. 2001. Eco-economy: building an economy for the earth. New York, NY: W.W. Norton & Company. 333 p.

Brown, L.R.; Kane, H. 1994. Full house: reassessing the earth's population carrying capacity. New York, NY: W. W. Norton & Company. 261 p.

Brown, Lester R. *et al.* 1994. State of the world 1994. New York, NY: W. W. Norton & Company. 265 p.

Burchell, R.W.; Listokin, D.; Galley, C.C. 2000. Smart growth: more than a ghost of urban policy past, less than a bold new horizon. Housing Policy Debate. 11(4): 821-879.

Chen, D.D.T. 2000. The science of smart growth. Scientific American. 283(6): 84-91.

Danielson, K.A.; Lang, R.E.; Fulton, W. 1999. What does smart growth mean for housing? Housing Facts & Findings. 1(3): 1, 12-15.

DeGrove, J.M. 1989. Growth management and governance. In: Brower, D.J.; Godschalk, D.R..; Porter, D.R., eds. Understanding growth management. Washington, DC: The Urban Land Institute: 22-36.

DeGrove, J.M.; Miness, D.A. 1992. The new frontier for land policy: planning and growth management in the states. Cambridge, MA: Lincoln Institute of Land Policy. 176 p.

Downs, A. 2001. What does 'smart growth' really mean? Planning. 67(4): 20-25.

Ehrlich, P.R.; Ehrlich, A.H. 1990. The population explosion. New York, NY: Simon and Schuster. 320 p.

Ehrlich, P.R.; Ehrlich, A.H. 1991. Healing the planet: strategies for resolving the environmental crisis. Reading, MA: Addison-Wesley Publishing Company, Inc. 366 p.

Finkler, E.; Peterson, D.L. 1974. Nongrowth planning strategies: the developing power of towns, cities, and regions. New York, NY: Praeger Publishers. 116 p.

Gann, J.L. 2004. The sound of music: orchestrating growth without sprawl. Planning & Zoning News. 22(5): 5-11.

Glickfield, M.; Levine, N. 1991. Growth controls: regional problems—local responses. Cambridge, MA: Lincoln Institute of Land Policy. 160 p.

Goodland, R. 1992. The case that the world has reached limits: more precisely that current throughput growth in the global economy cannot be sustained. Population and Environment. 13(2): 167-182.

Hall, P.; Pfeiffer, U. 2000. Urban future 21: a global agenda for twenty-first century cities. London, England: Spon Press. 363 p.

Howard, P.E. 1999. Report warns of state growth to 101 million. The Tampa Tribune. April 2, Friday: A2.

Kaiser, E.J.; Godschalk, D.R.; Chapin, F.S. 1995. Urban land use planning. 4th ed. Chicago, IL: University of Illinois Press. 493 p.

Kolankiewicz, L.; Beck, R. 2001. Weighing sprawl factors in large U.S. cities. Arlington, VA: SprawlCity. 63 p.

Krizek, K.J.; Power, J. 1996. A planners guide to sustainable development. Planning Advisory Service Report Number 467. Chicago, IL: American Planning Association. 66 p.

Landis, J.D. 1992. Do growth controls work? A new assessment. Journal of the American Planning Association. 58(4): 489-508.

Levy, J.M. 1994. Contemporary urban planning. Englewood Cliffs, NJ: Prentice Hall. 369 p.

Litman, T. 2003. Evaluating criticism of smart growth. Victoria, BC: Victoria Transport Policy Institute. 67 p. [Available online: http://www.vtpi.org/sgcritics.pdf]

Lorentz, A.; Shaw, K. 2000. Are you ready to bet on smart growth? Planning. 66(1): 4-9.

Lubchenco, J. *et al.* 1991. The sustainable biosphere initiative: an ecological research agenda. Ecology. 72(2): 371-412.

Manes, C. 1990. Green rage: radical environmentalism and the unmaking of civilization. Boston, MA: Little, Brown and Company. 291 p.

Mastny, L. 2002. World's coral reefs dying off. In: Worldwatch Institute. Vital signs 2002. New York, NY: W. W. Norton & Company: 92-106.

Meadows, D.H.; Meadows, D.L.; Randers, J. 1992. Beyond the limits: confronting global collapse, envisioning a sustainable future. Post Mills, VT: Chelsea Green Publishing Company. 300 p.

Meadows, D.H.; Meadows, D.L.; Randers, J.; Behrens, W.W. 1972. The limits to growth. New York, NY: Universe Books. 205 p.

Myers, R.A.; Worm, B. 2003. Letters to nature—rapid worldwide depletion of predatory fish communities. Nature. 423(6937): 280-283.

Nature Conservancy, The. 1997. The 1997 species report card: the state of U.S. plants and animals. Washington, DC: The Nature Conservancy. 52 p.

Nelson, A.C.; Duncan, J.B. 1995. Growth management principles and strategies. Chicago, IL: Planners Press. 172 p.

Noss, R.F.; LaRoe, E.T.; Scott, J.M. 1997. Endangered ecosystems of the United States: a preliminary assessment of loss and degradation. Washington, DC: Biological Resources Division, United States Geological Survey. 60 p.

Porter, D.R. 2002. Making smart growth work. Washington, DC: The Urban Land Institute. 175 p.

Postel, S. 1994. Carrying capacity: earth's bottom line. In: Brown, L.R. et al., ed. State of the world 1994. New York, NY: W. W. Norton & Company: 3-21.

Reilly, W.K., ed. 1973. The use of land: a citizens' policy guide to urban growth. New York, NY: Thomas Y. Crowell Co. 318 p.

Sawin, J.L. 2004. Making better energy choices. In: State of the world 2004. New York, NY: W. W. Norton & Company: 24-43.

Scott, R.W. 1975. Management and control of growth: an introduction and summary. In: Scott, R.W.; Brower, D.J.; Miner, D.D., eds. Management and control of growth: issues, techniques, problems and trends, vol. I. Washington, DC: The Urban Land Institute: 2-35.

Shearman, R. 1990. The meaning and ethics of sustainability. Environmental Management. 14(1): 1-8.

Smart Growth Network. 2002. Getting to smart growth: 100 policies for implementation. Washington, DC: International City/County Management Association. 97 p.

U.S. Department of Agriculture, Natural Resources Conservation Service. 2001. National resources inventory—2001 annual NRI: urbanization and development of rural land. Washington, DC: U.S. Department of Agriculture, Natural Resources Conservation Service. 4 p. [Available online: http://www.nrcs.usda.gov]

Van der Ryan, S.; Calthorpe, P. 1986. A new design synthesis for cities, suburbs, and towns: sustainable communities. San Francisco, CA: Sierra Club Books. 286 p.

Wackernagel, M.; Yount, J.D. 1998. The ecological footprint: an indicator of progress toward sustainability. Environmental Monitoring and Assessment. 51(1-2): 511-529.

Wackernagel, M. et al. 1997. Ecological footprints of nations: How much do they use? How much do they have? Toronto, Canada: International Council for Local Environmental Initiatives. 64 p.

Webb, M.; Jacobsen, J. 1982. U.S. carrying capacity: an introduction. Washington, DC: Carrying Capacity, Inc. 79 p.

Wheeler, S.M. 2000. Planning for metropolitan sustainability. Journal of Planning Education and Research. 20(2): 133-145.

Wilson, E. 1992. The diversity of life. Cambridge, MA: Harvard University Press. 424 p.

World Conservation Union. 2002. 2002 IUCN red list of threatened species. Gland, Switzerland: IUCN—World Conservation Union.

World Resources Institute. 1996. World resources 1996-97—the urban environment. Oxford, England: Oxford University Press. 365 p.

Worster, D. 1993. The wealth of nature: environmental history and the ecological imagination. New York, NY: Oxford University Press. 255 p.

WWF International. 2002. Living planet report 2002. Gland, Switzerland: World Wildlife Fund. 39 p. [Available online: http://www.panda.org]

Zovanyi, G. 1998. Growth management for a sustainable future: ecological sustainability as the new growth management focus of the 21st century. Westport, CT: Praeger Publishers. 221 p.

Zovanyi, G. 1999. The growth management delusion. Washington, DC: Negative Population Growth, Inc. 8 p. [Available online: http://www.npg.org]

Zovanyi, G. 2000. Growth management strategies for stopping growth in local communities. Washington, DC: Negative Population Growth, Inc. 12 p. [Available online: http://www.npg.org]

Zovanyi, G. 2004. A growth-management strategy for the Auckland region of New Zealand: pursuit of sustainability or mere growth accommodation? International Journal of Sustainable Development. 7(2): 121-145.

THE BIG TENT OF GROWTH MANAGEMENT: SMART GROWTH AS A MOVEMENT

Edward G. Goetz[1]

ABSTRACT—Growth management policies in the U.S. have failed to gain significant political support in many regions, limiting efforts to manage development patterns and protect natural resources. The Smart Growth movement has brought new voices into the debate over growth management and has provided a "big tent" under which transportation groups, environmentalists, advocates for affordable housing, and neighborhood activists have combined efforts to affect land policy. Although this has broadened political support for growth management, the Smart Growth movement still faces important challenges in unifying and mobilizing its diverse constituency.

Pinpointing the origins of the Smart Growth movement is difficult. Some argue that Smart Growth stems from the entire history of growth management efforts, going back as far as the Supreme Court's legitimization of zoning (Burchell *et al.* 2000). From this perspective, Smart Growth is merely a label for a repackaged assemblage of previous growth management techniques and is an evolutionary stage in the development of growth management approaches. A competing perspective is that Smart Growth brings together existing strategies in a new way, under the banner of a different set of growth management objectives, and it claims a much greater constituency for those strategies than ever before. According to this perspective, Smart Growth redefines earlier efforts, combines a variety of land-based interests not previously aligned with each other, and provides a unifying theoretical and political framework for the entire package.

In this paper I adopt the position that Smart Growth is an important break with previous growth management efforts and can be usefully examined as a separate movement. In fact, I argue that using the frameworks for the analysis of social and political movements clarifies much about Smart Growth as a phenomenon and assists in assessing the importance of the issue and its likelihood for political success.

ORIGINS OF THE SMART GROWTH MOVEMENT

The movement emerged in the mid-1990s, as several large institutional actors in urban development began to promote an alternative growth paradigm they came to call Smart Growth. Burchell *et al.* (2000) identified two initiatives that broke ground. The first—a combined effort of the American Planning Association (APA), the U.S. Department of Housing and Urban Development (HUD), and the Henry M. Jackson Foundation—aimed at updating local land use controls to emphasize more compact development patterns. This led to APA's "Growing Smarter" document, released in 1997. At about the same time, the Natural Resources Defense Council

(NRDC) and the Surface Transportation Policy Project (STPP) jointly developed what they called the Smart Growth Toolkit to assist local and state governments in producing walkable and transit-accessible development. In 1996, the U.S. Environmental Protection Agency (EPA) joined with nonprofit and government organizations to create the Smart Growth Network (SGN). Members of the SGN include a range of interest groups concerned with issues that range from the environment and historic preservation to real estate development and transportation. The ideas of these organizations were borrowed from the ideas of Peter Calthorpe (1993) and others about the benefits of compact development, transit-oriented urban forms, and what came to be called neotraditional neighborhood planning approaches.

The movement also was encouraged by the growing academic research on the issue of sprawl and the social and fiscal costs associated with sprawl (Katz 2002). A major study sponsored by the Transportation Research Board (Burchell *et al.* 1998) updated older work and pointed to a range of social and fiscal costs associated with sprawled development. Other academics and policy organizations also began to publish work on the costs of urban sprawl (see, for example, Beaumont 1994, Black 1996, Fodor 1997, Persky and Wiewel 1996).

Various policy-oriented and professional groups such as STPP, the Sierra Club, NRDC, and APA disseminated this new Smart Growth agenda by publishing reports and Web-based information. This emergent movement was able to accomplish a number of things in a relatively short period of time. The movement:

1. Defined a crisis by utilizing and synthesizing various research reports on the costs of sprawl.

2. Provided a framework for linking previously disparate concerns such as loss of farmland, traffic congestion, central city neighborhood decline, concentrated poverty, and even the growing problem of obesity.

[1] Urban and Regional Planning Program, Humphrey Institute of Public Affairs, University of Minnesota, 301 19th Avenue South, Minneapolis, MN 55455; e-mail: egoetz@umn.edu

Citation for proceedings: Bengston, David N., tech. ed. 2005. Policies for managing urban growth and landscape change: a key to conservation in the 21st Century. Gen. Tech. Rep. NC-265. St. Paul, MN: U.S. Department of Agriculture, Forest Service, North Central Research Station. 51 p.

3. Incorporated existing growth management techniques, adapting them to a slightly new policy agenda–moving from a concern about the amount of growth to a policy agenda focused on the quality of growth.

4. Combined these ideas into a single public policy paradigm, offering a new way of thinking about these old issues.

5. Achieved legislative successes at the state level, providing instant legitimacy, and offering a trial run for many of the concepts described in the Smart Growth agenda.

In a short period of time, the Smart Growth movement has become quite broad. One can find statements of support and evidence of activities on behalf of Smart Growth by a range of interests, including environmentalists, farmers, housing advocates, labor organizations, businesses, public health advocates, and even federal agencies. At the same time, however, the Smart Growth movement is a very shallow phenomenon in that it has no central identifiable constituency. Although a coalition of supporters does exist, there is no group of persons or organizations whose sense of identity is centrally connected to the issue. More problematic, there is no common set of grievances across all the members of the coalition.

THE BIG TENT

In its short history, the idea of Smart Growth has attracted a wide range of supporters. At the national level, first as Vice President and then as a Presidential candidate, Al Gore strongly supported a range of Smart Growth initiatives, primarily from an environmental standpoint. His Livability Agenda, launched in 1998, included initiatives to ease traffic congestion, preserve green space, and pursue regional Smart Growth strategies. Yet notable members of the Republican party and the Bush administration also have Smart Growth credentials, from former EPA administrator Christine Whitman to former Transportation Secretary Norman Mineta. The Bush administration's EPA has been a highly visible supporter of Smart Growth.

The business community also has become involved in Smart Growth advocacy. Business groups in Oregon, Kentucky, Georgia, Michigan, and Rhode Island have undertaken efforts to promote Smart Growth and curb sprawl (Seth 2000). These groups suggest that Smart Growth is a pro-growth strategy that allows regions to rationally develop and minimize the labor costs associated with rising housing costs and rising transportation costs and commuting times.

At the same time, labor groups also have supported Smart Growth. A 2003 study by the national nonprofit Good Jobs First found that regions with growth controls actually benefited from nearly a third more construction jobs than areas without such policies (Mattera and LeRoy 2003). Although these findings may reflect the fact that more economically dynamic (and therefore growing) metropolitan areas are more likely to impose Smart Growth controls than are stagnant regions, labor officials have concluded that growth controls do not necessarily limit jobs (Ritter 2004): "Union leaders

also say Smart Growth enriches their members' lives by producing less traffic, cleaner air, shorter commutes and more open space" (p. 2).

Historic preservation activists support Smart Growth for its emphasis on redevelopment and rehabilitation of older structures and older settlements. Environmentalists and transit activists are, of course, central actors in the Smart Growth coalition. Advocates for affordable housing support Smart Growth because they favor the redevelopment of older neighborhoods and the mixing of income within new residential areas. Central city neighborhood organizations support Smart Growth because they favor brownfield redevelopment and improvements to declining urban infrastructure called for by the movement. Farmers support efforts to preserve agricultural land, and public health organizations point to the health problems associated with sprawl. Even the Union for Reform Judaism has supported Smart Growth because of its potential to narrow the gap between the affluent and the poor, which, the organization maintains, is in line with Judaism's tenet of *tikkun olam* (repairing the world).[2]

SMART GROWTH AS A MOVEMENT

How do we characterize the Smart Growth movement and therefore, how do we study it? Theory related to social movements suggests that a classic movement exhibits a set of characteristics that do not particularly match the Smart Growth case. The classic theory suggests the importance of spontaneous, collective action on the part of a group, emphasizing social change-oriented goals. Such action, according to the theory, arises from deeply felt deprivation or the existence of a social crisis. This theory assumes, then, a mass constituency for the movement, and ultimately, one that self-identifies as such (as exemplified, for example, by the civil rights movement, the labor movement, or the women's movement). The theory also emphasizes the extra-institutional actions of this mass constituency. That is, the movement emerges as a response to governmental or institutional neglect of core concerns of the constituency. Such movements are typically political outsiders restricted to outsider political strategies such as protest actions, sit-ins, marches, and the like. Such strategies build solidarity while creating greater awareness of group grievances.

It is difficult to align this model of social movements with the Smart Growth case. First, there is difficulty in identifying the constituency for this movement. Where is the group of people self-identifying as Smart Growth supporters? And where do we look for the evidence of their mass mobilization? We know, perhaps, that some Smart Growth supporters are commuters dissatisfied with the amount of time they spend in their cars. Some are farmers concerned about the encroachment of residential development. Some are environmentalists concerned about the loss of habitat and the degradation of natural resources. But there is as yet little, if any, degree of collective consciousness among these groups sufficient to produce a mass mobilization.

---

[2] From a resolution considered by the membership of the Union of American Hebrew Congregations in 1999; http://www.urj.us/orlando/preso/growth.shtml, accessed April 20, 2005.

Second, there is no evidence that these groups experience the same set of grievances. To the contrary, the wrong that each group feels is quite particular to its situation. There is no common crisis, at least at the level of felt experience between farmers and advocates for affordable housing or between many of the other groups that support Smart Growth. Although one might generalize and argue that sprawled development and the costs of this development is the common experience, a social movement requires that the constituent members define their grievances in collective terms. Smart Growth supporters, even the most active, do not collectively define their grievances the way the labor movement could focus on working conditions or the civil rights movement could focus on discrimination and segregation. That is, farmers support Smart Growth for one set of reasons, while housing advocates express support for a separate set, and labor has a third set of reasons. Such a situation can broaden support for the issue, but it does not provide the basis for an active political movement. Indeed, such a situation might even impede the development of an active political movement to the extent that there are areas of conflict among the various groups in support of Smart Growth and their reasons for supporting it. One example of this is the potential conflict between environmentalists, on the one hand, who see Smart Growth as a means of protecting more environmentally sensitive lands, and housing advocates, on the other hand, who look to Smart Growth to provide more affordable housing opportunities.

In response, Smart Growth advocates have attempted to create a common understanding of Smart Growth that bridges the often wide gap between coalition members. Much of this work is aimed at substituting the concept of "sprawl" as a unifying concern for various other problems (traffic congestion, loss of habitat and farmland) that tend to emphasis more particularistic problems. Such a collective consciousness might well strengthen the movement, but it is not clear the extent to which these efforts have been or will be successful. In any case, this collective consciousness is one of the objectives of the movement, not its genesis.

McCarthy and Zald (1973, 1976) broadened the analytic field in social movements to include what they call "professionalized" social movements. As Staggenborg (1988: 585) wrote,

> In contrast to what they term "classical" movement organizations, which rely on the mass mobilization of "beneficiary" constituents as active participants, "professional" social movement organizations rely primarily on paid leaders and "conscience" constituents who contribute money and are paper members rather than active participants... "Entrepreneurs" can mobilize sentiments into movement organizations without the benefit of precipitating events or "suddenly imposed major grievances"... and without established constituencies.

This formulation gets closer to the Smart Growth experience. It does away with the need for a mobilized constituency group or for a triggering event or grievance. It also identifies the role of "professionals" or "entrepreneurs" in generating a movement. Yet, at the same time, the McCarthy and Zald theory does assume that the work of the professionals is to induce a mass movement, to induce a constituency with a collective

consciousness. In this respect, the professional movement is a type of first stage that gives way at some point to mass politics.

Perhaps most useful to an understanding of Smart Growth as a movement is what Rochon (1998) called a "critical community." Critical communities form around a particular issue or problem and provide the foundation for further development of a movement. Specifically, Rochon argued:

> The creation of new ideas occurs initially within a relatively small community of critical thinkers who have developed a sensitivity to some problem, an analysis of the sources of the problem, and a prescription for what should be done about the problem. These critical thinkers do not necessarily belong to a formally constituted organization, but they are part of a self-aware, mutually interacting group (p. 22).

Critical communities are composed of scientists, academics, and social and policy analysts who provide a new or unique analysis of a social problem that serves as the basis for a new movement. As Rochon (1998: 23) argued, "critical communities seek acceptance of a new conceptualization of a problem–they want to make sure that other people 'get it.'"

Although seen as the first stage in a nascent political or social movement, critical communities can have direct impact on cultural values, public policy, or both. Depending partly on the political and cultural status of members of the critical community and in part on the receptivity of the political system to new policy demands (Rochon 1998), critical communities may quickly succeed in pressing for new public policy. This is a fairly accurate description of the dynamics surrounding Smart Growth. The critical community that emerged around the issue of Smart Growth in the 1990s included groups with both high status and significant political influence. This led to the relatively quick adoption of Smart Growth solutions in a number of states and the continued dissemination of Smart Growth information.

Godschalk (2000) claimed that more than one-half of the state-of-the-state addresses by the nation's governors in 2000 discussed Smart Growth. Salkin (2002) documented gubernatorial action on Smart Growth in over 30 states, involving both Republican and Democratic officials. Republican governors in Florida, Illinois, Arizona, and elsewhere created executive branch initiatives to study and coordinate Smart Growth activities. Legislatures in Colorado, Iowa, and Wisconsin enacted Smart Growth bills of one type or another in the early years of this decade.

In Michigan, for example, established land-based interest groups such as the Michigan Land Use Institute (with more than 2,500 member-families, organizations, businesses, and local governments) and a statewide interdenominational congregation-based organization played key roles in establishing a Smart Growth approach. The W.K. Kellogg Foundation has funded research that led to the publication of "*Local Smart Growth Actions to Combat Sprawl,*" a guide to local governments interested in implementing Smart Growth.

In some states, much progress was made in the 1990s. In Maryland, the declining health of Chesapeake Bay, as documented by the U.S. Environmental Protection Agency, was the triggering mechanism for statewide planning legislation in 1992. A subsequent assessment of the 1992 legislation led to a statewide series of public meetings and forums in 1996, organized by the office of then new Governor Parris Glendening. These meetings resulted in the landmark Maryland Smart Growth Initiatives, enacted in 1997.

Despite the ability of critical communities to have immediate impact, they too exist as a prelude to a more mass mobilization in the development of a social or political movement dynamic. Although critical communities offer innovative ways of thinking about social problems and solutions, they give way ultimately to a grassroots activism in what Rochon (1998) called a two-stage process of value generation and value diffusion. If the first stage is the redefinition of social problems and solutions by the critical community, the second stage is the introduction of those innovations into wider society. In the second stage, "the ideas of the critical community are reshaped by leaders and activists in social and political movements, in accord with the demands of mobilization and the experience of movement struggle. Once the issue becomes public, the movement takes center stage and the critical community fades to the background" (Rochon 1998: 95).

This suggests that the transition from the actions of a critical community to the emergence of a bonafide political or social movement is of vital importance. At least two conditions make such a transition easier. The first is the degree to which there is unity within the critical community, and the second is the degree to which there is a basis for group identification among activists. The Smart Growth movement may be deficient on at least the second criterion.

As Rubin (1994: 14, quoted in Rochon 1998: 23) noted, "agreement that there are problems does not mean there is agreement on what those problems are, or on what makes them problems, or on what to do about them." This is particularly a potential problem in the Smart Growth movement because it attracts such disparate interests. The wide range of Smart Growth supporters is not a cohesive group, nor are they entirely comfortable with each other. Environmentalists and advocates for affordable housing often clash at the level of specific projects because they may represent a tradeoff between affordability and environmental protection. Obviously, business and labor have antagonistic interests that hinder their ability to coalesce around Smart Growth. There is even significant disagreement within some of the groups, notably agricultural interests, about the wisdom of Smart Growth.

As a result, even the common identification of sprawl as a problem does not guarantee a unified movement or agreed-upon policy response. As Gearin (2004: 293) found in her study of southern California, even though "Southern California jurisdictions, policy bodies, and politicians have hopped on the smart growth bandwagon... [the] different proponents articulate different interpretations of smart growth" that have inhibited the development of a coherent policy movement.

Thus, in spite of specific legislative and administrative accomplishments, in spite of a wide range of interest groups expressing support for the idea of Smart Growth, the Smart Growth coalition may not be able to make the important transition from critical community to political/social movement. Can the Smart Growth movement sustain itself? This question is made all the more important by a pattern of declining media attention. Figure 1 presents data on print-media news stories about Smart Growth.

Two patterns emerge from the data. First, media interest peaks in the early part of this decade and then declines. Second, regions vary in the salience of the issue. The metropolitan area of Atlanta, one of the most sprawling in the country, is the setting for an extensive discussion of Smart Growth as judged by the frequency of news stories in the region's leading newspaper.

Figure 1.—News stories about Smart Growth in five U.S. cities.

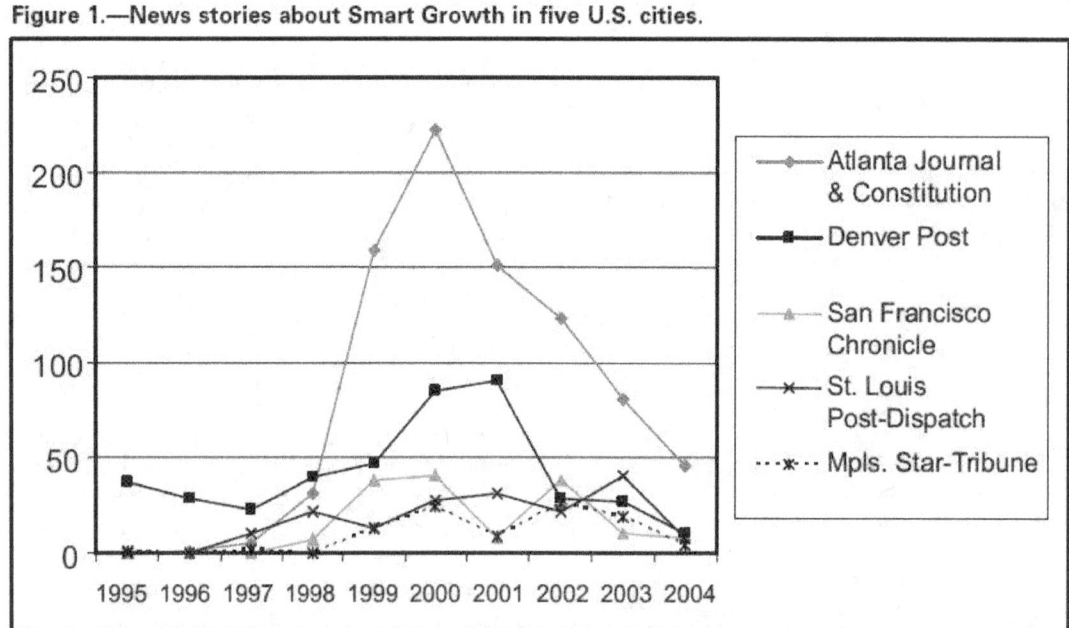

Denver had the second most frequent mention and preceded Atlanta in its interest in the topic with over 100 stories already printed between 1995 and 1998. The other metropolitan areas have shown a much lower level of interest in the topic.

To this point, I have argued that Smart Growth has little potential for emerging as a broad-based social or political movement. Following Iyengar and Kinder (1987), it is unlikely that Smart Growth will emerge as a movement because the issue is not experienced as both a personal and a group predicament. This is due primarily to the low capacity for this movement to create strong solidarities (Rochon 1998: 128). Such solidarities are more easily created when group members share ascriptive traits that easily communicate membership status or form the basis of a common social experience to which members react. For Smart Growth to emerge as a real political movement, it needs to make the transition from the critical community's value generation stage to the value diffusion stage identified by Rochon in which the principles of Smart Growth are translated by leaders into the concerns and the work of citizen activists. In the next section, I examine one way in which this might occur. I use the Smart Growth Organizing Project (SGOP) of Minnesota as a case example of a community organizing around the principles of Smart Growth.

THE SMART GROWTH ORGANIZING PROJECT

The Smart Growth movement, to date, has largely been an insider campaign involving high-status governmental and private sector organizations. Furthermore, the movement has been political in a narrow sense, focusing on altering governmental actions in the area of land use regulation and regional development policy. The Smart Growth Organizing Project (SGOP) of Minnesota is a conscious attempt to move Smart Growth activities beyond the fairly self-contained policy circles in which most of the debate has been located. In the process, advocates in Minnesota are pursuing a tiered approach to Smart Growth objectives, by complementing the work of insider groups at the level of policymaking with an organizing strategy aimed at mobilizing a broad range of supporters at the community level.

In 2001, the McKnight Foundation (a member of the Smart Growth Funders' Network) sponsored a series of Smart Growth Dialogues that brought together representatives from a number of local and statewide organizations and public agencies working on growth issues. Over a number of months the group created an advocacy strategy aimed at both achieving policy changes in the state and building a movement around Smart Growth principles.

The group split into four Smart Growth sectors, each dealing with a separate domain of Smart Growth issues: transportation, open space, land use regulation, and housing.[3]

Within each of these sectors, the participants were asked to strategize around three different approaches: a policy and regulatory approach that focused on necessary changes to state and local policies, a demonstration projects tactic that identified specific development projects that could be pursued and used as examples of successful Smart Growth, and finally an education and engagement emphasis to build grassroots community support for Smart Growth. Finally, specific actions needed for each of the approaches (policy and regulatory, demonstration projects, and education and engagement) were identified at three scales: state, regional, and local. Thus the sector groups created a matrix to identify specific action steps necessary at the intersection of these three scales.

The pursuit of the policy and the demonstration strategies largely could be carried out by the same group of organizations, specifically those that were lobbying organizations or operational agencies already oriented toward the work of making, changing, and implementing public policy. This group made up the State Policy Group, which later became known as the Minnesota Smart Growth Network. The other group of participants, those whose organizations were more membership-based and focused on grassroots efforts, formed the Organizing Project (SGOP) to work on the education and engagement strategies. These two metagroups constituted a conscious attempt to follow a two-tiered approach to building the Smart Growth movement. The Smart Growth Network would continue to focus on transmitting the Smart Growth message to policymakers and public officials, while the organizing project would engage in grassroots mobilization of residents throughout the Twin Cities metropolitan region and, to a somewhat lesser extent, statewide.

SGOP was charged with turning Smart Growth into a grassroots political movement, something that had not been achieved yet in any region of the country, even in those regions that had produced the landmark legislation. Short of that, SGOP was responsible for at least finding a consistent grassroots source of support for specific Smart Growth issues and demonstration projects.

SGOP hired a professional organizer and located its staff member at the offices of the Alliance for Metropolitan Stability, a membership based organization working on regional equity issues. The SGOP organizer conducted more than 50 individual meetings with community group leaders throughout the metropolitan area and convened roundtable meetings for organizers. These meetings were, according to the SGOP organizer, "a place to come and talk to each other about organizing, and to build skills." These meetings were also meant to communicate the principles of "Smart Growth as we define it."

---

[3] The transportation group consisted of Minnesotans for an Energy-Efficient Economy, Transit for Livable Communities, Minnesota Center for Environmental Advocacy, and the Center for Neighborhoods. The Housing sector was the Family Housing Fund, Greater Minnesota Housing Fund, Minnesota Housing Partnership, Minneapolis Consortium of Community Developers, Twin Cities Local Initiatives Support Corporation, and Metropolitan Interfaith Coalition for Affordable Housing. The Open Space group was the Minnesota Land Trust, Friends of the Mississippi River, Friends of the Minnesota Valley, and 1000 Friends of Minnesota. The Land Use group, which renamed itself the Metropolitan Growth Strategies group, was made up of the Design Center for the American Urban Landscape, the Alliance for Metropolitan Stability, the Metropolitan Council of the Twin Cities, and the North Metro Mayors Association.

The distinctive way in which SGOP defines Smart Growth is laid out in the organization's statement of principles. While attempting to increase public understanding of growth issues and enhancing the capacity of local organizing around growth issues, SGOP chose racial and class equity as a central value in its work. The organization states that a central value in its work is:

> Confronting issues of race, privilege, culture, and ethnicity and developing a strong understanding about how these issues and disparities manifest themselves within growth and development policies and decisions throughout the region. This includes: Developing greater comfort and skill in confronting issues of race, privilege, culture, and ethnicity. Ensuring that low-income neighborhoods and communities of color are decision makers about growth. Embracing growth strategies that promote racial, economic, environmental and ethnic equity.[4]

Although race and class equity is only one of seven different values identified in the SGOP document, it is a cornerstone of the group's work. SGOP understands that this approach takes Smart Growth in a new direction. But, the SGOP organizer says, "the traditional Smart Growth movement has not addressed the race and class issues, but we have some common cause with these groups." SGOP sees itself as "the edgier" side of the Smart Growth movement. "We don't connect much with the Smart Growth Network. I don't have much success meeting with those people. They do work on a broader policy level. I work on building a power base."

SGOP attempts to build that power base through campaigns that focus on specific issues throughout the metropolitan area. Initially, the SGOP steering committee identified four campaigns to become involved in. The first was to create a grassroots coalition to support the creation of a dedicated fund for transit in the state. This issue had been circulating among "policy wonks" for some time, according to the SGOP organizer, and SGOP wanted to create a political base for the idea. The transit trust fund is modeled after the fund for highways that exists at the federal level, and like the highway fund it is aimed at providing a steady stream of revenue dedicated for a single purpose–the development of transit throughout the state. In this effort, unlike the three that follow, SGOP is the lead organization, working with one of its member groups to pressure the legislature to act.

The second campaign was an attempt to prevent the demolition of high-density low-cost housing in a Minneapolis suburb. This effort was a reaction to the creation of a "density reduction taskforce" in Brooklyn Park that recommended the demolition of more than 700 units of affordable rental housing in a single neighborhood. The city had tried to remove this housing in a redevelopment project some years earlier, but the financing for the deal had fallen through. SGOP was attracted to this issue because of the avowed purpose of reducing housing density in one of the few places where high-density housing can be said to exist in the suburbs of the Twin Cities and because of the unstated objective of eliminating low-cost housing inhabited primarily by people of color. SGOP joined

with several housing advocacy groups to mobilize residents to attend public meetings and to contact local officials and the news media in an effort to stop the demolition. The advocates ultimately prevailed when the citizens of Brooklyn Park defeated a ballot referendum to raise the revenues necessary for the demolition and redevelopment.

The third SGOP campaign was to join a battle in another northern suburb over a proposed transit-oriented development (TOD) at a proposed commuter rail stop. The North Star commuter rail is a proposed line running from Minneapolis through its northwest suburbs to St. Cloud, Minnesota. The project has been the subject of much debate at the legislature and has had inconsistent support from the legislature and the governor's office over the past 5 years. Nevertheless, planning is underway for the proposed stops along the route. One of those is the Riverdale stop in Coon Rapids, Minnesota. A shopping center already exists on the land, which is owned by the county. Advocates are working with the county redevelopment authority on a TOD that would include affordable workforce housing. The City of Coon Rapids, on the other hand, is offering density bonuses for upscale housing. SGOP's objectives in this campaign are not only to ensure a high-density TOD at the site, but also to get as much affordable housing built there as possible. SGOP is helping suburban organizers influence the Coon Rapids city council.

The last of the four campaigns also involves a possible TOD along a proposed rail line, this one a light-rail stop in St. Paul. Here the city has professed a willingness to create a TOD in what is now a low-density commercial area. The developer, however, is threatening to go in a different direction, and SGOP is working with a local community organization to pack the public hearings and demand a "smarter" development plan.

THE CHALLENGES OF BUILDING A SMART GROWTH MOVEMENT

Smart Growth advocates in Minnesota have taken a distinctive approach to building a Smart Growth movement. They have in one sense acknowledged the structural imperative of supporting the work of the critical community (the Minnesota Smart Growth Network) with a mobilization effort aimed at translating new policy solutions into the concerns of a grassroots movement. They have pursued a two-tiered approach that includes roughly parallel efforts at both of these levels. Yet, according to SGOP itself, there is little communication between these parallel movements. SGOP has come to its own definition of Smart Growth and shaped an organizing strategy around that definition. The two tiers of this movement work in relative isolation from each other. Whether this is sustainable in the long run depends in part on the consistency of vision between SGOP and the Smart Growth Network.

SGOP's focus on racial/class equity, although a part of the Smart Growth agenda as defined by most national organizations (see, for example, EPA, NRDC), is nevertheless, one of the more contentious political elements of that agenda. SGOP has chosen a difficult issue around which to frame its organizing work. In the Minneapolis-St. Paul metropolitan area, as in most metropolitan areas, there is political tension on issues of

---

[4] Smart Growth Organizing Project (no date). SGOP statement of values. Available from author.

race and class equity. The organization has eschewed a strategy that might have identified a less contentious common grievance related to unplanned development (such as declining quality of life).

The SGOP mobilization model is an attempt to connect Smart Growth with existing organizations by using a campaign approach. Whether this approach can build a consistent constituency across issue areas is yet to be determined. For its part, SGOP admits the potential for turf battles between groups that are part of the larger Smart Growth coalition. Conflicts between the agendas of environmentalists and advocates for affordable housing, for example, "crop up a lot in the work we do," she said. She argues, however, that their organizing efforts, built around specific issues, are the best way to work on turf issues and barriers to working together. "We want to reduce those barriers, to be the movement's therapist," said SGOP's lead organizer. "In specific instances people can work through their issues [with each other]. That is one of the benefits of the trust that was established in the working roundtables and skill-building sessions we ran early on."

The structure of the Smart Growth movement in Minnesota is one means of facing the movement's challenges and could, if effective, serve as a national model. As in other places, a critical community emerged during the late 1990s, led by policy groups and funded by interested foundations. The bridge between that community and a grassroots mobilization is represented by the work of SGOP. It is too early to judge whether this two-tiered approach can accomplish its goals. For now, advocates are gambling that it can.

LITERATURE CITED

Beaumont, C. 1994. How superstore sprawl can harm communities–and what citizens can do about it. Washington, DC: National Trust for Historic Preservation. 120 p.

Black, J.T. 1996. The economics of sprawl. Urban Land. 55(3): 6-52.

Burchell, R.W.; Listokin, D.; Galley, C.C. 2000. Smart Growth: more than a ghost of urban policy past, less than a bold new horizon. Housing Policy Debate. 11(4): 821- 879.

Burchell, R.W.; Shad, N.A.; Listokin, D.; *et al.* 1998. The costs of sprawl–revisited. Report 39. Transit Cooperative Research Program, Transportation Research Board, National Research Council. Washington, DC: National Academy Press. 268 p.

Calthorpe, P. 1993. The next American metropolis: ecology, community and the American dream. Princeton, NJ: Princeton University Press. 175 p.

Fodor, E.V. 1997. The real cost of growth in Oregon. Population and Environment. 18(4): 373-388.

Gearin, E. 2004. Smart Growth or Smart Growth machine? The Smart Growth Movement and its implications. In: Wolch, J.; Pastor Jr., M.; Dreier, P. Eds. Up against the sprawl: public policy and the making of Southern California. Minneapolis, MN: University of Minnesota Press: 279-307.

Godschalk, D.R. 2000. Smart Growth efforts around the nation. Popular Government. Vol. 12, Fall, page 13.

Iyengar, S.; Kinder, D.R. 1987. News that matters: television and American opinion. Chicago, IL: University of Chicago Press. 187 p.

Katz, B. 2002. Smart Growth: the future of the American metropolis? Center for the Analysis of Social Exclusion (CASE) paper 58. London: London School of Economics. 32 p.

Mattera, P., with G. LeRoy. 2003. The jobs are back in town: urban Smart Growth and construction employment. Washington, DC: Good Jobs First. 56 p.

McCarthy, J.D.; Zald, M.N. 1973. The trend of social movements in America: professionalization and resource mobilization. Morristown, NJ: General Learning Press. 30 p.

McCarthy, J.D.; Zald, M.N. 1976. Resource mobilization and social movements: a partial theory. American Journal of Sociology. 82: 1212-41.

National Association of Local Government Environmental Professionals, and Smart Growth Leadership Institute. 2004. Smart Growth is smart business: boosting the bottom line and community prosperity. Washington, DC: NALGEP. 60 p.

Persky, J.; Wiewel, W. 1996. Central city and suburban development: who pays and who benefits? Chicago, IL: Great Cities Institute, University of Illinois. 17 p.

Ritter, J. 2004. Unions seeing new benefits in "smart growth." USA Today. January 1, page 2A.

Rochon, T.R. 1998. Culture moves: ideas, activism, and changing values. Princeton, NJ: Princeton University Press. 282 p.

Rubin, C. 1994. The green crusade: rethinking the roots of environmentalism. New York: Free Press. 312 p.

Salkin, P.E. 2002. The Smart Growth agenda: a snapshot of state activity at the turn of the century. Saint Louis University Public Law Review. 21: 271.

Staggenborg, S. 1997. The consequences of professionalization and formalization in the pro-choice movement. In: McAdam, D.; Snow, D.A., eds. Social movements: readings on their emergence, mobilization and dynamics. Los Angeles, CA: Roxbury Publishing Company: 421-439.

MISSION STATEMENT

We believe the good life has its roots in clean air, sparkling water, rich soil, healthy economies and a diverse living landscape. Maintaining the good life for generations to come begins with everyday choices about natural resources. The North Central Research Station provides the knowledge and the tools to help people make informed choices. That's how the science we do enhances the quality of people's lives.

For further information contact:

 North Central
Research Station
USDA Forest Service
1992 Folwell Ave., St. Paul, MN 55108

Or visit our web site:
www.ncrs.fs.fed.us